BRET HARTE
—*From the Original Painting by John Pettie. R. A.*

"ARGONAUT EDITION" OF
THE WORKS OF BRET HARTE

CONDENSED NOVELS

NEW BURLESQUES

BY

BRET HARTE

ILLUSTRATED

VIGILANS ET AUDAX

P. F. COLLIER & SON
NEW YORK

HANDSOME IS AS HANDSOME DOES.

By CH——S R——DE.

CHAPTER I.

THE Dodds were dead. For twenty year they had slept under the green graves of Kittery churchyard The townfolk still spoke of them kindly. The keeper of the alehouse, where David had smoked his pipe, regretted him regularly, and Mistress Kitty, Mrs. Dodd's maid, whose trim figure always looked well in her mistress's gowns, was inconsolable. The Hardins were in America. Raby was aristocratically gouty ; Mrs. Raby, religious. Briefly, then, we have disposed of —

1. Mr. and Mrs. Dodd (dead).

2. Mr. and Mrs. Hardin (translated).

3. Raby, *baron et femme.* (Yet I don't know about the former ; he came of a long-lived family, and the gout is an uncertain disease.)

We have active at the present writing (*place aux dames*) —

1. Lady Caroline Coventry, niece of Sir Frederick.

2. Faraday Huxley Little, son of Henry and Grace Little, deceased.

Sequitur to the above, A HERO AND HEROINE.

CHAPTER II.

ON the death of his parents, Faraday Little was taken to Raby Hall. In accepting his guardianship, Mr. Raby struggled stoutly against two prejudices: Faraday was plain-looking and sceptical.

"Handsome is as handsome does, sweetheart," pleaded Jael, interceding for the orphan with arms that were still beautiful. "Dear knows, it is not his fault if he does not look like — his father," she added with a great gulp. Jael was a woman, and vindicated her womanhood by never entirely forgiving a former rival.

"It 's not that alone, madam," screamed Raby,

" but, d——m it, the little rascal 's a scientist, — an atheist, a radical, a scoffer ! Disbelieves in the Bible, ma'am ; is full of this Darwinian stuff about natural selection and descent.   Descent, for-sooth ! In my day, madam, gentlemen were con-tent to trace their ancestors back to gentlemen, and not to — monkeys ! "

" Dear heart, the boy is clever," urged Jael.

" Clever ! " roared Raby ; " what does a gentle-man want with cleverness ? "

CHAPTER III.

YOUNG Little *was* clever. At seven he had constructed a telescope ; at nine, a flying-ma-chine. At ten he saved a valuable life.

Norwood Park was the adjacent estate, — a lordly domain dotted with red deer and black trunks, but scrupulously kept with gravelled roads as hard and blue as steel. There Little was stroll-ing one summer morning, meditating on a new top with concealed springs. At a little distance before him he saw the flutter of lace and ribbons.

A young lady, a very young lady, — say of seven summers, — tricked out in the crying abominations of the present fashion, stood beside a low bush. Her nursery-maid was not present, possibly owing to the fact that John the footman was also absent.

Suddenly Little came towards her. "Excuse me, but do you know what those berries are?" He was pointing to the low bush filled with dark clusters of shining — suspiciously shining — fruit.

"Certainly; they are blueberries."

"Pardon me; you are mistaken. They belong to quite another family."

Miss Impudence drew herself up to her full height (exactly three feet nine and a half inches), and, curling an eight of an inch of scarlet lip, said, scornfully, "*Your* family, perhaps."

Faraday Little smiled in the superiority of boyhood over girlhood.

"I allude to the classification. That plant is the belladonna, or deadly nightshade. Its alkaloid is a narcotic poison."

Sauciness turned pale. "I — have — just — eaten — some!" And began to whimper. "O dear, what shall I do?" Then did it, i. e. wrung her small fingers and cried.

"Pardon me one moment." Little passed his arm around her neck, and with his thumb opened widely the patrician-veined lids of her sweet blue eyes. " Thank Heaven, there is yet no dilation of the pupil ; it is not too late !" He cast a rapid glance around. The nozzle and about three feet of garden hose lay near him.

"Open your mouth, quick !"

It was a pretty, kissable mouth. But young Little meant business. He put the nozzle down her pink throat as far as it would go.

"Now, don't move."

He wrapped his handkerchief around a hoop-stick. Then he inserted both in the other end of the stiff hose. It fitted snugly. He shoved it in and then drew it back.

Nature abhors a vacuum. The young patrician was as amenable to this law as the child of the lowest peasant.

She succumbed. It was all over in a minute. Then she burst into a small fury.

"You nasty, bad — *ugly* boy."

Young Little winced, but smiled.

"Stimulants," he whispered to the frightened

nursery-maid who approached; " good evening."
He was gone.

CHAPTER IV.

THE breach between young Little and Mr. Raby
was slowly widening.   Little found objectionable
features in the Hall.   " This black oak ceiling and
wainscoating is not as healthful as plaster; besides, it absorbs the light.   The bedroom ceiling
is too low ; the Elizabethan architects knew nothing of ventilation.   The color of that oak panel-
ling which you admire is due to an excess of car-
bon and the exuvia from the pores of your
skin — "

" Leave the house," bellowed Raby, " before the
roof falls on your sacrilegious head ! "

As Little left the house, Lady Caroline and a
handsome boy of about Little's age entered.   Lady
Caroline recoiled, and then — blushed.   Little
glared; he instinctively felt the presence of a
rival.

CHAPTER V.

LITTLE worked hard. He studied night and day. In five years he became a lecturer, then a professor.

He soared as high as the clouds, he dipped as low as the cellars of the London poor. He analyzed the London fog, and found it two parts smoke, one disease, one unmentionable abominations. He published a pamphlet, which was violently attacked. Then he knew he had done something.

But he had not forgotten Caroline. He was walking one day in the Zoölogical Gardens and he came upon a pretty picture, — flesh and blood too.

Lady Caroline feeding buns to the bears! An exquisite thrill passed through his veins. She turned her sweet face and their eyes met. They recollected their first meeting seven years before, but it was his turn to be shy and timid. Wonderful power of age and sex! She met him with perfect self-possession.

"Well meant, but indigestible I fear" (he alluded to the buns).

"A clever person like yourself can easily correct that" (she, the slyboots, was thinking of something else).

In a few moments they were chatting gayly. Little eagerly descanted upon the different animals; she listened with delicious interest. An hour glided delightfully away.

After this sunshine, clouds.

To them suddenly entered Mr. Raby and a handsome young man. The gentlemen bowed stiffly and looked vicious, — as they felt. The lady of this quartette smiled amiably, as she did not feel.

"Looking at your ancestors, I suppose," said Mr. Raby, pointing to the monkeys; "we will not disturb you. Come." And he led Caroline away.

Little was heart-sick. He dared not follow them. But an hour later he saw something which filled his heart with bliss unspeakable.

Lady Caroline, with a divine smile on her face, feeding the monkeys!

CHAPTER VI.

ENCOURAGED by love, Little worked hard upon his new flying-machine. His labors were lightened by talking of the beloved one with her French maid Thérèse, whom he had discreetly bribed. Mademoiselle Thérèse was venal, like all her class, but in this instance I fear she was not bribed by British gold. Strange as it may seem to the British mind, it was British genius, British eloquence, British thought, that brought her to the feet of this young *savan.*

"I believe," said Lady Caroline, one day, interrupting her maid in a glowing eulogium upon the skill of " M. Leetell," — " I believe you are in love with this Professor." A quick flush crossed the olive cheek of Thérèse, which Lady Caroline afterward remembered.

The eventful day of trial came. The public were gathered, impatient and scornful as the pigheaded public are apt to be. In the open area a long cylindrical balloon, in shape like a Bologna sausage, swayed above the machine, from which, like some enormous bird caught in a net, it tried to free itself. A heavy rope held it fast to the ground.

Little was waiting for the ballast, when his eye caught Lady Caroline's among the spectators. The glance was appealing. In a moment he was at her side.

" I should like so much to get into the machine," said the arch-hypocrite, demurely.

" Are you engaged to marry young Raby," said Little, bluntly.

" As you please," she said with a courtesy; " do I take this as a refusal ? "

Little was a gentleman. He lifted her and her lapdog into the car.

" How nice ! it won't go off ? "

" No, the rope is strong, and the ballast is not yet in."

A report like a pistol, a cry from the spectators, a thousand hands stretched to grasp the parted rope, and the balloon darted upward.

Only one hand of that thousand caught the rope, — Little's ! But in the same instant the horror-stricken spectators saw him whirled from his feet and borne upward, still clinging to the rope, into space.

CHAPTER VII.*

LADY CAROLINE fainted. The cold watery nose of her dog on her cheek brought her to herself. She dared not look over the edge of the car; she dared not look up to the bellying monster above her, bearing her to death. She threw herself on the bottom of the car, and embraced the only living thing spared her, — the poodle. Then she cried. Then a clear voice came apparently out of the circumambient air : —

"May I trouble you to look at the barometer?"

She put her head over the car. Little was hanging at the end of a long rope. She put her head back again.

In another moment he saw her perplexed, blushing face over the edge, — blissful sight.

* The right of dramatization of this and succeeding chapters is reserved by the writer.

"O, please don't think of coming up! Stay there, do!"

Little stayed. Of course she could make nothing out of the barometer, and said so. Little smiled.

"Will you kindly send it down to me?"

But she had no string or cord. Finally she said, "Wait a moment."

Little waited. This time her face did not appear. The barometer came slowly down at the end of — a stay-lace.

The barometer showed a frightful elevation. Little looked up at the valve and said nothing. Presently he heard a sigh. Then a sob. Then, rather sharply, —

"Why don't you do something?"

CHAPTER VIII.

LITTLE came up the rope hand over hand. Lady Caroline crouched in the farther side of the car. Fido, the poodle, whined. "Poor thing," said Lady Caroline, "it's hungry."

" Do you wish to save the dog?" said Little.

" Yes."

" Give me your parasol."

She handed Little a good-sized affair of lace and silk and whalebone. (None of your "sun-shades.") Little examined its ribs carefully.

" Give me the dog."

Lady Caroline hurriedly slipped a note under the dog's collar, and passed over her pet.

Little tied the dog to the handle of the parasol and launched them both into space. The next moment they were slowly, but tranquilly, sailing to the earth.

" A parasol and a parachute are distinct, but not different.   Be not alarmed, he will get his dinner at some farm-house."

" Where are we now ? "

" That opaque spot you see is London fog. Those twin clouds are North and South America. Jerusalem and Madagascar are those specks to the right.

Lady Caroline moved nearer ; she was becoming interested.   Then she recalled herself and said freezingly, " How are we going to descend ? "

" By opening the valve."

" Why don't you open it then ? "

" BECAUSE THE VALVE-STRING IS BROKEN ! "

CHAPTER IX.

LADY CAROLINE fainted. When she revived it was dark. They were apparently cleaving their way through a solid block of black marble. She moaned and shuddered.

" I wish we had a light."

" I have no lucifers," said Little. " I observe, however, that you wear a necklace of amber. Amber under certain conditions becomes highly electrical. Permit me."

He took the amber necklace and rubbed it briskly. Then he asked her to present her knuckle to the gem. A bright spark was the result. This was repeated for some hours. The light was not brilliant, but it was enough for the purposes of propriety, and satisfied the delicately minded girl.

Suddenly there was a tearing, hissing noise and a smell of gas. Little looked up and turned pale. The balloon, at what I shall call the pointed end of the Bologna sausage, was evidently bursting from increased pressure. The gas was escaping, and already they were beginning to descend. Little was resigned but firm.

" If the silk gives way, then we are lost. Unfortunately I have no rope nor material for binding it."

The woman's instinct had arrived at the same conclusion sooner than the man's reason. But she was hesitating over a detail.

" Will you go down the rope for a moment ? " she said, with a sweet smile.

Little went down. Presently she called to him. She held something in her hand, — a wonderful invention of the seventeenth century, improved and perfected in this : a pyramid of sixteen circular hoops of light yet strong steel, attached to each other by cloth bands.

With a cry of joy Little seized them, climbed to the balloon, and fitted the elastic hoops over its conical end. Then he returned to the car.

"We are saved."

Lady Caroline, blushing, gathered her slim but antique drapery against the other end of the car.

CHAPTER X.

THEY were slowly descending. Presently Lady Caroline distinguished the outlines of Raby Hall. "I think I will get out here," she said.

Little anchored the balloon and prepared to follow her.

"Not so, my friend," she said, with an arch smile. "We must not be seen together. People might talk. Farewell."

Little sprang again into the balloon and sped away to America. He came down in California, oddly enough in front of Hardin's door, at Dutch Flat. Hardin was just examining a specimen of ore.

"You are a scientist; can you tell me if that is worth anything?" he said, handing it to Little.

Little held it to the light. " It contains ninety per cent of silver."

Hardin embraced him. " Can I do anything for you, and why are you here ? "

Little told his story. Hardin asked to see the rope. Then he examined it carefully.

" Ah, this was cut, not broken ! "

" With a knife ? " asked Little.

" No. Observe both sides are equally indented. It was done with a *scissors !* "

" Just Heaven ! " gasped Little. " Thérèse ! "

CHAPTER XI.

LITTLE returned to London. Passing through London one day he met a dog-fancier. " Buy a nice poodle, sir ? "

Something in the animal attracted his attention. " Fido !" he gasped.

The dog yelped.

Little bought him. On taking off his collar a piece of paper rustled to the floor. He knew the handwriting and kissed it. It ran : —

"To the Hon. Augustus Raby:— I cannot marry you. If I marry any one" (sly puss) "it will be the man who has twice saved my life, — Professor Little.

"Caroline Coventry."

And she did.

LOTHAW;

OR,

THE ADVENTURES OF A YOUNG GENTLEMAN IN SEARCH OF A RELIGION.

By MR. BENJAMINS.

CHAPTER I.

" I REMEMBER him a little boy," said the Duchess. " His mother was a dear friend of mine ; you
know she was one of my bridesmaids."

" And you have never seen him since, mamma ? "
asked the oldest married daughter, who did not
look a day older than her mother.

" Never ; he was an orphan shortly after. I
have often reproached myself, but it is so difficult
to see boys."

This simple yet first-class conversation existed
in the morning-room of Plusham, where the mistress of the palatial mansion sat involved in the
sacred privacy of a circle of her married daughters. One dexterously applied golden knitting-

needles to the fabrication of a purse of floss silk
of the rarest texture, which none who knew the
almost fabulous wealth of the Duke would believe was ever destined to hold in its silken
meshes a less sum than £ 1,000,000 ; another
adorned a slipper exclusively with seed pearls ; a
third emblazoned a page with rare pigments and
the finest quality of gold leaf. Beautiful forms
leaned over frames glowing with embroidery, and
beautiful frames leaned over forms inlaid with
mother-of-pearl. Others, more remote, occasionally burst into melody as they tried the passages
of a new and exclusive air given to them in MS.
by some titled and devoted friend, for the private
use of the aristocracy alone, and absolutely pro-
hibited for publication.

The Duchess, herself the superlative of beauty,
wealth, and position, was married to the highest
noble in the Three Kingdoms. Those who talked
about such matters said that their progeny were
exactly like their parents, — a peculiarity of the
aristocratic and wealthy. They all looked like
brothers and sisters, except their parents, who,
such was their purity of blood, the perfection of

their manners, and the opulence of their condition, might have been taken for their own children's elder son and daughter. The daughters, with one exception, were all married to the highest nobles in the land. That exception was the Lady Coriander, who, there being no vacancy above a marquis and a rental of £1,000,000, waited. Gathered around the refined and sacred circle of their breakfast-table, with their glittering coronets, which, in filial respect to their father's Tory instincts and their mother's Ritualistic tastes, they always wore on their regal brows, the effect was dazzling as it was refined. It was this peculiarity and their strong family resemblance which led their brother-in-law, the good-humored St. Addlegourd, to say that, " 'Pon my soul, you know, the whole precious mob looked like a ghastly pack of court cards, you know." St. Addlegourd was a radical. Having a rent-roll of £15,000,000, and belonging to one of the oldest families in Britain, he could afford to be.

" Mamma, I 've just dropped a pearl," said the Lady Coriander, bending over the Persian hearth-rug.

"From your lips, sweet friend," said Lothaw, who came of age and entered the room at the same moment.

"No, from my work. It was a very valuable pearl, mamma; papa gave Isaacs and Sons £ 50,000 for the two."

"Ah, indeed," said the Duchess, languidly rising; "let us go to luncheon."

"But your Grace," interposed Lothaw, who was still quite young, and had dropped on all-fours on the carpet in search of the missing gem, "consider the value — "

"Dear friend," interposed the Duchess, with infinite tact, gently lifting him by the tails of his dress-coat, "I am waiting for your arm."

CHAPTER II.

LOTHAW was immensely rich. The possessor of seventeen castles, fifteen villas, nine shooting-boxes, and seven town houses, he had other estates of which he had not even heard.

Everybody at Plusham played croquet, and

none badly. Next to their purity of blood and great wealth, the family were famous for this accomplishment. Yet Lothaw soon tired of the game, and after seriously damaging his aristocratically large foot in an attempt to "tight croquet" the Lady Aniseed's ball, he limped away to join the Duchess.

"I 'm going to the hennery," she said.

"Let me go with you, I dearly love fowls — broiled," he added, thoughtfully.

"The Duke gave Lady Montairy some large Cochins the other day," continued the Duchess, changing the subject with delicate tact.

> " Lady Montairy,
> Quite contrairy,
> How do your Cochins grow ? "

sang Lothaw gayly.

The Duchess looked shocked. After a prolonged silence, Lothaw abruptly and gravely said : —

"If you please, ma'am, when I come into my property I should like to build some improved dwellings for the poor, and marry Lady Coriander."

"You amaze me, dear friend, and yet both your aspirations are noble and eminently proper," said the Duchess; "Coriander is but a child, — and yet," she added, looking graciously upon her companion, "for the matter of that, so are you."

CHAPTER III.

MR. PUTNEY GILES'S was Lothaw's first grand dinner-party. Yet, by carefully watching the others, he managed to acquit himself creditably, and avoided drinking out of the finger-bowl by first secretly testing its contents with a spoon. The conversation was peculiar and singularly interesting.

"Then you think that monogamy is simply a question of the thermometer?" said Mrs. Putney Giles to her companion.

"I certainly think that polygamy should be limited by isothermal lines," replied Lothaw.

"I should say it was a matter of latitude," observed a loud talkative man opposite. He was an Oxford Professor with a taste for satire, and had made himself very obnoxious to the company, during dinner, by speaking disparagingly of a former well-known Chancellor of the Exchequer, — a great statesman and brilliant novelist, — whom he feared and hated.

Suddenly there was a sensation in the room; among the females it absolutely amounted to a nervous thrill. His Eminence, the Cardinal, was announced. He entered with great suavity of manner, and, after shaking hands with everybody, asking after their relatives, and chucking the more delicate females under the chin with a high-bred grace peculiar to his profession, he sat down, saying, "And how do we all find ourselves this evening, my dears?" in several different languages, which he spoke fluently.

Lothaw's heart was touched. His deeply religious convictions were impressed. He instantly went up to this gifted being, confessed, and received absolution. "To-morrow," he said to himself, " I will partake of the communion, and endow the Church with my vast estates. For the present I 'll let the improved cottages go."

CHAPTER IV.

As Lothaw turned to leave the Cardinal, he was struck by a beautiful face. It was that of a matron, slim but shapely as an Ionic column. Her face was Grecian, with Corinthian temples; Hellenic eyes that looked from jutting eyebrows, like dormer-windows in an Attic forehead, completed her perfect Athenian outline. She wore a black frock-coat tightly buttoned over her bloomer trousers, and a standing collar.

"Your Lordship is struck by that face," said a social parasite.

"I am; who is she?"

"Her name is Mary Ann. She is married to an American, and has lately invented a new religion."

"Ah!" said Lothaw eagerly, with difficulty restraining himself from rushing toward her.

"Yes; shall I introduce you?"

Lothaw thought of Lady Coriander's High Church proclivities, of the Cardinal, and hesitated: "No, I thank you, not now."

CHAPTER V.

Lᴏᴛʜᴀw was maturing. He had attended two
woman's rights conventions, three Fenian meet-
ings, had dined at White's, and had danced *vis-à-
vis* to a prince of the blood, and eaten off of gold
plates at Crecy House.

His stables were near Oxford, and occupied
more ground than the University. He was driv-
ing over there one day, when he perceived some
rustics and menials endeavoring to stop a pair
of runaway horses attached to a carriage in which
a lady and gentleman were seated. Calmly awaiting the termination of the accident, with high-
bred courtesy Lothaw forbore to interfere until
the carriage was overturned, the occupants thrown
out, and the runaways secured by the servants,
when he advanced and offered the lady the exclusive use of his Oxford stables.

Turning upon him a face whose perfect Hellenic
details he remembered, she slowly dragged a gentleman from under the wheels into the light and

presented him with ladylike dignity as her husband, Major-General Camperdown, an American.

"Ah," said Lothaw, carelessly, "I believe I have some land there. If I mistake not, my agent, Mr. Putney Giles, lately purchased the State of — Illinois — I think you call it."

"Exactly. As a former resident of the city of Chicago, let me introduce myself as your tenant."

Lothaw bowed graciously to the gentleman, who, except that he seemed better dressed than most Englishmen, showed no other signs of inferiority and plebeian extraction.

"We have met before," said Lothaw to the lady as she leaned on his arm, while they visited his stables, the University, and other places of interest in Oxford. "Pray tell me, what is this new religion of yours?"

"It is Woman Suffrage, Free Love, Mutual Affinity, and Communism. Embrace it and me."

Lothaw did not know exactly what to do. She however soothed and sustained his agitated frame and sealed with an embrace his speechless form. The General approached and coughed slightly with gentlemanly tact.

" My husband will be too happy to talk with
you further on this subject," she said with quiet
dignity, as she regained the General's side.
" Come with us to Oneida. Brook Farm is a
thing of the past."

CHAPTER VI.

As Lothaw drove toward his country-seat, " The
Mural Enclosure," he observed a crowd, apparently
of the working class, gathered around a singular-
looking man in the picturesque garb of an Ethio-
pian serenader. " What does he say ? " inquired
Lothaw of his driver.

The man touched his hat respectfully and said,
" My Mary Ann."

" ' My Mary Ann ! ' " Lothaw's heart beat rapidly. Who was this mysterious foreigner ? He
had heard from Lady Coriander of a certain
Popish plot ; but could he connect Mr. Camperdown with it ?

The spectacle of two hundred men at arms who
advanced to meet him at the gates of The Mural

Enclosure drove all else from the still youthful
and impressible mind of Lothaw. Immediately
behind them, on the steps of the baronial halls,
were ranged his retainers, led by the chief cook
and   bottle-washer,   and   head   crumb-remover.
On either side were two companies of laundry-
maids, preceded by the chief crimper and fluter,
supporting a long Ancestral Line, on which de-
pended the family linen, and under which the
youthful lord of the manor passed into the halls
of his fathers.   Twenty-four scullions carried the
massive gold and silver plate of the family on
their shoulders, and deposited it at the feet of their
master.   The spoons were then solemnly counted
by the steward, and the perfect ceremony ended.

Lothaw sighed.   He sought out the gorgeously
gilded " Taj," or sacred mausoleum erected to his
grandfather in the second story front room, and
wept over the man he did not know.   He wan-
dered alone in his magnificent park, and then,
throwing himself on a grassy bank, pondered on
the Great First Cause, and the necessity of religion.   " I will send Mary Ann a handsome present," said Lothaw, thoughtfully.

CHAPTER VII.

"EACH of these pearls, my Lord, is worth fifty thousand guineas," said Mr. Amethyst, the fashionable jeweler, as he lightly lifted a large shovelful from a convenient bin behind his counter.

"Indeed," said Lothaw, carelessly, "I should prefer to see some expensive ones."

"Some number sixes, I suppose," said Mr. Amethyst, taking a couple from the apex of a small pyramid that lay piled on the shelf. "These are about the size of the Duchess of Billingsgate's, but they are in finer condition. The fact is, her Grace permits her two children, the Marquis of Smithfield and the Duke of St. Giles, — two sweet pretty boys, my Lord, — to use them as marbles in their games. Pearls require some attention, and I go down there regularly twice a week to clean them. Perhaps your Lordship would like some ropes of pearls ?"

"About half a cable's length," said Lothaw, shortly, "and send them to my lodgings."

Mr. Amethyst became thoughtful. " I am afraid I have not the exact number — that is — excuse me one moment. I will run over to the Tower and borrow a few from the crown jewels." And before Lothaw could prevent him, he seized his hat and left Lothaw alone.

His position certainly was embarrassing. He could not move without stepping on costly gems which had rolled from the counter; the rarest diamonds lay scattered on the shelves; untold fortunes in priceless emeralds lay within his grasp. Although such was the aristocratic purity of his blood and the strength of his religious convictions that he probably would not have pocketed a single diamond, still he could not help thinking that he might be accused of taking some. " You can search me, if you like," he said when Mr. Amethyst returned; " but I assure you, upon the honor of a gentleman, that I have taken nothing."

" Enough, my Lord," said Mr. Amethyst, with a low bow; " we never search the aristocracy."

CHAPTER VIII.

As Lothaw left Mr. Amethyst's, he ran against General Camperdown. " How is Mary Ann ? " he asked hurriedly.

" I regret to state that she is dying," said the General, with a grave voice, as he removed his cigar from his lips, and lifted his hat to Lothaw.

" Dying ! " said Lothaw, incredulously.

" Alas, too true ! " replied the General. " The engagements of a long lecturing season, exposure in travelling by railway during the winter, and the imperfect nourishment afforded by the refresh- ments along the road, have told on her delicate frame. But she wants to see you before she dies. Here is the key of my lodging. I will finish my cigar out here."

Lothaw hardly recognized those wasted Hellenic outlines as he entered the dimly lighted room of the dying woman. She was already a classic ruin, — as wrecked and yet as perfect as the Parthenon. He grasped her hand silently.

2--v. 5

" Open-air speaking twice a week, and saleratus bread in the rural districts, have brought me to this," she said feebly; "but it is well. The cause progresses. The tyrant man succumbs."

Lothaw could only press her hand.

" Promise me one thing. Don't — whatever you do — become a Catholic."

" Why ? "

" The Church does not recognize divorce. And now embrace me. I would prefer at this supreme moment to introduce myself to the next world through the medium of the best society in this. Good by. When I am dead, be good enough to inform my husband of the fact."

CHAPTER IX.

LOTHAW spent the next six months on an Aryan island, in an Aryan climate, and with an Aryan race.

" This is an Aryan landscape," said his host, " and that is a Mary Ann statue." It was, in fact, a full-length figure in marble of Mrs. General Camperdown !

"If you please, I should like to become a Pagan," said Lothaw, one day, after listening to an impassioned discourse on Greek art from the lips of his host.

But that night, on consulting a well-known spiritual medium, Lothaw received a message from the late Mrs. General Camperdown, advising him to return to England. Two days later he presented himself at Plusham.

"The young ladies are in the garden," said the Duchess. "Don't you want to go and pick a rose?" she added with a gracious smile, and the nearest approach to a wink that was consistent with her patrician bearing and aquiline nose.

Lothaw went and presently returned with the blushing Coriander upon his arm.

"Bless you, my children," said the Duchess. Then, turning to Lothaw, she said: "You have simply fulfilled and accepted your inevitable destiny. It was morally impossible for you to marry out of this family. For the present, the Church of England is safe."

MUCK-A-MUCK.

A MODERN INDIAN NOVEL.

AFTER COOPER.

———◆———

CHAPTER I.

IT was toward the close of a bright October day. The last rays of the setting sun were reflected from one of those sylvan lakes peculiar to the Sierras of California. On the right the curling smoke of an Indian village rose between the columns of the lofty pines, while to the left the log cottage of Judge Tompkins, embowered in buckeyes, completed the enchanting picture.

Although the exterior of the cottage was humble and unpretentious, and in keeping with the wildness of the landscape, its interior gave evidence of the cultivation and refinement of its inmates. An aquarium, containing goldfishes, stood on a marble centre-table at one end of the apartment, while a magnificent grand piano occupied the other. The floor was covered with a yielding tapestry carpet, and the walls were adorned with paintings from the pencils of Van Dyke, Rubens, Tintoretto, Michael Angelo, and the productions of the more modern Turner, Kensett, Church, and Bierstadt. Although Judge Tompkins had chosen the frontiers of civilization as his home, it was impossible for him to entirely forego the habits and tastes of his former life. He was seated in a luxurious arm-chair, writing at a mahogany *écritoire*, while his daughter, a lovely young girl of seventeen summers, plied her crochet-needle on an ottoman beside him. A bright fire of pine logs flickered and flamed on the ample hearth.

Genevra Octavia Tompkins was Judge Tompkins's only child. Her mother had long since died on the Plains. Reared in affluence, no pains had been spared with the daughter's education. She was a graduate of one of the principal seminaries, and spoke French with a perfect Benicia accent. Peerlessly beautiful, she was dressed in a white *moire antique* robe trimmed with *tulle*. That simple rosebud, with which most heroines

exclusively decorate their hair, was all she wore
in her raven locks.

The Judge was the first to break the silence.

"Genevra, the logs which compose yonder fire
seem to have been incautiously chosen. The sibila-
tion produced by the sap, which exudes copiously
therefrom, is not conducive to composition."

"True, father, but I thought it would be prefer-
able to the constant crepitation which is apt to
attend the combustion of more seasoned ligneous
fragments."

The Judge looked admiringly at the intellectual
features of the graceful girl, and half forgot the
slight annoyances of the green wood in the musical accents of his daughter. He was smoothing her
hair tenderly, when the shadow of a tall figure,
which suddenly darkened the doorway, caused him
to look up.

CHAPTER II.

IT needed but a glance at the new-comer to detect at once the form and features of the haughty
aborigine, — the untaught and untrammelled son

of the forest. Over one shoulder a blanket, neg-
ligently but gracefully thrown, disclosed a bare and
powerful breast, decorated with a quantity of three-
cent postage-stamps which he had despoiled from
an Overland Mail stage a few weeks previous. A
cast-off beaver of Judge Tompkins's, adorned by a
simple feather, covered his erect head, from beneath which his straight locks descended. His
right hand hung lightly by his side, while his
left was engaged in holding on a pair of pantaloons, which the lawless grace and freedom of
his lower limbs evidently could not brook.

"Why," said the Indian, in a low sweet tone, —
"why does the Pale Face still follow the track of
the Red Man? Why does he pursue him, even
as *O-kee-chow*, the wild-cat, chases *Ka-ka*, the
skunk? Why are the feet of *Sorrel-top*, the
white chief, among the acorns of *Muck-a-Muck*,
the mountain forest? Why," he repeated, quietly
but firmly abstracting a silver spoon from the
table, — "why do you seek to drive him from the
wigwams of his fathers? His brothers are already
gone to the happy hunting-grounds. Will the
Pale Face seek him there?" And, averting his

face from the Judge, he hastily slipped a silver cake-basket beneath his blanket, to conceal his emotion.

"*Muck-a-Muck* has spoken," said Genevra, softly. "Let him now listen. Are the acorns of the mountain sweeter than the esculent and nutritious bean of the Pale Face miner? Does my brother prize the edible qualities of the snail above that of the crisp and oleaginous bacon? Delicious are the grasshoppers that sport on the hillside, — are they better than the dried apples of the Pale Faces? Pleasant is the gurgle of the torrent, *Kish-Kish*, but is it better than the cluck-cluck of old Bourbon from the old stone bottle?"

"Ugh!" said the Indian, — "ugh! good. The White Rabbit is wise. Her words fall as the snow on Tootoonolo, and the rocky heart of Muck-a-Muck is hidden. What says my brother the Gray Gopher of Dutch Flat?"

"She has spoken, Muck-a-Muck," said the Judge, gazing fondly on his daughter. "It is well. Our treaty is concluded. No, thank you, — you need *not* dance the Dance of Snow Shoes, or the Moccasin Dance, the Dance of Green Corn, or the

Treaty Dance. I would be alone. A strange sad-
ness overpowers me."

"I go," said the Indian. "Tell your great chief
in Washington, the Sachem Andy, that the Red
Man is retiring before the footsteps of the adventurous Pioneer. Inform him, if you please, that
westward the star of empire takes its way, that
the chiefs of the Pi-Ute nation are for Recon-
struction to a man, and that Klamath will poll a
heavy Republican vote in the fall."

And folding his blanket more tightly around
him, Muck-a-Muck withdrew.

CHAPTER III.

GENEVRA TOMPKINS stood at the door of the log-
cabin, looking after the retreating Overland Mail
stage which conveyed her father to Virginia City.
"He may never return again," sighed the young
girl as she glanced at the frightfully rolling vehicle
and wildly careering horses, — "at least, with unbroken bones. Should he meet with an accident!
I mind me now a fearful legend, familiar to my

childhood.   Can it be that the drivers on this line
are privately instructed to despatch all passengers
maimed by accident, to prevent tedious litigation ?
No, no.   But why this weight upon my heart ? "

She seated herself at the piano and lightly
passed her hand over the keys.   Then, in a clear
mezzo-soprano voice, she sang the first verse of one
of the most popular Irish ballads : —

> " O *Arrah*, *ma dheelish*, the distant *dudheen*
> Lies soft in the moonlight, *ma bouchal vourneen :*
> The springing *gossoons* on the heather are still,
> And the *caubeens* and *colleens* are heard on the hills."

But as the ravishing notes of her sweet voice
died upon the air, her hands sank listlessly to her
side.   Music could not chase away the mysterious
shadow from her heart.   Again she rose.   Putting
on a white crape bonnet, and carefully drawing a
pair of lemon-colored gloves over her taper fingers,
she seized her parasol and plunged into the depths
of the pine forest.

CHAPTER IV.

GENEVRA had not proceeded many miles before
a weariness seized upon her fragile limbs, and she
would fain seat herself upon the trunk of a pros-
trate pine, which she previously dusted with her
handkerchief. The sun was just sinking below
the horizon, and the scene was one of gorgeous
and sylvan beauty. "How beautiful is Nature!"
murmured the innocent girl, as, reclining gracefully against the root of the tree, she gathered up
her skirts and tied a handkerchief around her
throat. But a low growl interrupted her medita-
tion. Starting to her feet, her eyes met a sight
which froze her blood with terror.

The only outlet to the forest was the narrow
path, barely wide enough for a single person,
hemmed in by trees and rocks, which she had
just traversed. Down this path, in Indian file,
came a monstrous grizzly, closely followed by a
California lion, a wild-cat, and a buffalo, the rear
being brought up by a wild Spanish bull. The

mouths of the three first animals were distended
with frightful significance; the horns of the last
were lowered as ominously. As Genevra was preparing to faint, she heard a low voice behind her.

"Eternally dog-gone my skin ef this ain't the
puttiest chance yet."

At the same moment, a long, shining barrel
dropped lightly from behind her, and rested over
her shoulder.

Genevra shuddered.

"Dern ye — don't move!"

Genevra became motionless.

The crack of a rifle rang through the woods.
Three frightful yells were heard, and two sullen
roars. Five animals bounded into the air and
five lifeless bodies lay upon the plain. The well-
aimed bullet had done its work. Entering the
open throat of the grizzly, it had traversed his
body only to enter the throat of the California
lion, and in like manner the catamount, until it
passed through into the respective foreheads of
the bull and the buffalo, and finally fell flattened
from the rocky hillside.

Genevra turned quickly. "My preserver!" she

shrieked, and fell into the arms of Natty Bumpo, the celebrated Pike Ranger of Donner Lake.

CHAPTER V.

THE moon rose cheerfully above Donner Lake. On its placid bosom a dug-out canoe glided rapidly, containing Natty Bumpo and Genevra Tompkins.

Both were silent. The same thought possessed each, and perhaps there was sweet companionship even in the unbroken quiet. Genevra bit the handle of her parasol and blushed. Natty Bumpo took a fresh chew of tobacco. At length Genevra said, as if in half-spoken revery: —

" The soft shining of the moon and the peaceful ripple of the waves seem to say to us various things of an instructive and moral tendency."

"You may bet yer pile on that, Miss," said her companion, gravely. " It 's all the preachin' and psalm-singin' I 've heern since I was a boy."

" Noble being!" said Miss Tompkins to herself, glancing at the stately Pike as he bent over his paddle to conceal his emotion. "Reared in this wild seclusion, yet he has become penetrated with visible consciousness of a Great First Cause." Then, collecting herself, she said aloud: "Methinks 't were pleasant to glide ever thus down the stream of life, hand in hand with the one being whom the soul claims as its affinity. But what am I saying?" — and the delicate-minded girl hid her face in her hands.

A long silence ensued, which was at length broken by her companion.

"Ef you mean you 're on the marry," he said, thoughtfully, "I ain't in no wise partikler!"

"My husband," faltered the blushing girl; and she fell into his arms.

In ten minutes more the loving couple had landed at Judge Tompkins's.

CHAPTER VI.

A YEAR has passed away. Natty Bumpo was returning from Gold Hill, where he had been to purchase provisions. On his way to Donner Lake, rumors of an Indian uprising met his ears. " Dern their pesky skins, ef they dare to touch my Jenny," he muttered between his clenched teeth.

It was dark when he reached the borders of the lake. Around a glittering fire he dimly discerned dusky figures dancing. They were in war paint. Conspicuous among them was the renowned Muck-a-Muck. But why did the fingers of Natty Bumpo tighten convulsively around his rifle?

The chief held in his hand long tufts of raven hair. The heart of the pioneer sickened as he recognized the clustering curls of Genevra. In a moment his rifle was at his shoulder, and with a sharp "ping," Muck-a-Muck leaped into the air a corpse. To knock out the brains of the remaining savages, tear the tresses from the stiffening hand of Muck-a-Muck, and dash rapidly forward to the cottage of Judge Tompkins, was the work of a moment.

He burst open the door. Why did he stand transfixed with open mouth and distended eye-balls? Was the sight too horrible to be borne? On the contrary, before him, in her peerless beauty, stood Genevra Tompkins, leaning on her father's arm.

"Ye 'r not scalped, then !" gasped her lover.

"No. I have no hesitation in saying that I am not; but why this abruptness?" responded Genevra.

Bumpo could not speak, but frantically produced the silken tresses. Genevra turned her face aside.

"Why, that 's her waterfall!" said the Judge.

Bumpo sank fainting to the floor.

The famous Pike chieftain never recovered from the deceit, and refused to marry Genevra, who died, twenty years afterwards, of a broken heart. Judge Tompkins lost his fortune in Wild Cat. The stage passes twice a week the deserted cottage at Donner Lake. Thus was the death of Muck-a-Muck avenged.

TERENCE DENVILLE.

By CH—L—S L—V—R.

———◆———

CHAPTER I.

MY HOME.

THE little village of Pilwiddle is one of the smallest and obscurest hamlets on the western coast of Ireland. On a lofty crag, overlooking the hoarse Atlantic, stands "Denville's Shot Tower" — a corruption by the peasantry of *D'Enville's Château*, so called from my great-grandfather, Phelim St. Remy d'Enville, who assumed the name and title of a French heiress with whom he ran away. To this fact my familiar knowledge and excellent pronunciation of the French language may be attributed, as well as many of the events which covered my after life.

The Denvilles were always passionately fond of field sports. At the age of four, I was already the boldest rider and the best shot in the country.

When only eight, I won the St. Remy Cup at the Pilwiddle races, — riding my favorite bloodmare *Hellfire.* As I approached the stand amidst the plaudits of the assembled multitude, and cries of, " Thrue for ye, Masther Terence," and " O, but it 's a Dinville ! " there was a slight stir among the gentry, who surrounded the Lord Lieutenant, and other titled personages whom the race had attracted thither. " How young he is, — a mere child ; and yet how noble-looking," said a sweet low voice, which thrilled my soul.

I looked up and met the full liquid orbs of the Hon. Blanche Fitzroy Sackville, youngest daughter of the Lord Lieutenant. She blushed deeply. I turned pale and almost fainted. But the cold, sneering tones of a masculine voice sent the blood back again into my youthful cheek.

" Very likely the ragged scion of one of these banditti Irish gentry, who has taken naturally to ' the road.' He should be at school — though I warrant me his knowledge of Terence will not extend beyond his own name," said Lord Henry Somerset, aid-de-camp to the Lord Lieutenant.

A moment and I was perfectly calm, though

cold as ice. Dismounting, and stepping to the side of the speaker, I said in a low, firm voice : —

"Had your Lordship read Terence more carefully, you would have learned that banditti are sometimes proficient in other arts beside horsemanship," and I touched his holster significantly with my hand. I had not read Terence myself, but with the skilful audacity of my race I calculated that a vague allusion, coupled with a threat, would embarrass him. It did.

"Ah — what mean you ? " he said, white with rage.

"Enough, we are observed," I replied ; "Father Tom will wait on you this evening ; and to-morrow morning, my lord, in the glen below Pilwiddle we will meet again."

"Father Tom — glen ! " ejaculated the Englishman, with genuine surprise. "What ? do priests carry challenges and act as seconds in your infernal country ? "

"Yes ! " I answered, scornfully, "why should they not ? Their services are more often necessary than those of a surgeon," I added significantly, turning away.

The party slowly rode off, with the exception of the Hon. Blanche Sackville, who lingered for a moment behind. In an instant I was at her side. Bending her blushing face over the neck of her white filly, she said hurriedly : —

"Words have passed between Lord Somerset and yourself. You are about to fight. Don't deny it — but hear me. You will meet him — I know your skill of weapons. He will be at your mercy. I entreat you to spare his life!"

I hesitated. "Never!" I cried passionately; "he has insulted a Denville!"

"Terence," she whispered, "Terence — *for my sake?*"

The blood rushed to my cheeks, and her eyes sought the ground in bashful confusion.

"You love him then?" I cried, bitterly.

"No, no," she said, agitatedly, "no, you do me wrong. I — I — cannot explain myself. My father! — the Lady Dowager Sackville — the estate of Sackville — the borough — my uncle, Fitzroy Somerset. Ah! what am I saying? Forgive me. O Terence," she said, as her beautiful head sank on my shoulder, "you know not what I suffer!"

I seized her hand and covered it with passionate kisses. But the high-bred English girl, recovering something of her former *hauteur,* said hastily, "Leave me, leave me, but promise!"

"I promise," I replied, enthusiastically; "I *will* spare his life!"

"Thanks, Terence, — thanks!" and disengaging her hand from my lips she rode rapidly away.

The next morning, the Hon. Captain Henry Somerset and myself exchanged nineteen shots in the glen, and at each fire I shot away a button from his uniform. As my last bullet shot off the last button from his sleeve, I remarked quietly, "You seem now, my lord, to be almost as ragged as the gentry you sneered at," and rode haughtily away.

CHAPTER II.

THE FIGHTING FIFTY-SIXTH.

WHEN I was nineteen years old my father sold the *Château d'Enville* and purchased my commission in the "Fifty-sixth" with the proceeds. "I say, Denville," said young McSpadden, a boy-

faced ensign, who had just joined, "you 'll repre-
sent the estate in the Army, if you won't in the
House." Poor fellow, he paid for his meaningless
joke with his life, for I shot him through the
heart the next morning. " You 're a good fellow,
Denville," said the poor boy faintly, as I knelt beside him: "good by!" For the first time since
my grandfather's death I wept. I could not help
thinking that I would have been a better man if
Blanche — but why proceed ? Was she not now
in Florence — the belle of the English Embassy ?

But Napoleon had returned from Elba. Europe
was in a blaze of excitement. The Allies were
preparing to resist the Man of Destiny. We were
ordered from Gibraltar home, and were soon again
en route for Brussels. I did not regret that I was
to be placed in active service. I was ambitious,
and longed for an opportunity to distinguish myself. My garrison life in Gibraltar had been
monotonous and dull. I had killed five men in
duel, and had an affair with the colonel of my
regiment, who handsomely apologized before the
matter assumed a serious aspect. I had been
twice in love. Yet these were but boyish freaks
and follies. I wished to be a man.

The time soon came, — the morning of Waterloo. But why describe that momentous battle, on which the fate of the entire world was hanging? Twice were the Fifty-sixth surrounded by French cuirassiers, and twice did we mow them down by our fire. I had seven horses shot under me, and was mounting the eighth, when an orderly rode up hastily, touched his cap, and, handing me a despatch, galloped rapidly away.

I opened it hurriedly and read: —

" LET PICTON ADVANCE IMMEDIATELY ON THE RIGHT."

I saw it all at a glance. I had been mistaken for a general officer. But what was to be done? Picton's division was two miles away, only accessible through a heavy cross fire of artillery and musketry. But my mind was made up.

In an instant I was engaged with an entire squadron of cavalry, who endeavored to surround me. Cutting my way through them, I advanced boldly upon a battery and sabred the gunners before they could bring their pieces to bear. Looking around, I saw that I had in fact penetrated the French centre. Before I was well aware of

the locality, I was hailed by a sharp voice in
French, —

"Come here, sir!"

I obeyed, and advanced to the side of a little
man in a cocked hat.

"Has Grouchy come?"

"Not yet, sire," I replied, — for it was the
Emperor.

"Ha!" he said suddenly, bending his piercing
eyes on my uniform; "a prisoner?"

"No, sire," I said, proudly.

"A spy?"

I placed my hand upon my sword, but a gesture
from the Emperor bade me forbear.

"You are a brave man," he said.

I took my snuff-box from my pocket, and, taking a pinch, replied by handing it, with a bow, to
the Emperor.

His quick eye caught the cipher on the lid.

"What! a D'Enville? Ha! this accounts for
the purity of your accent. Any relation to
Roderick d'Enville?"

"My father, sire."

"He was my schoolfellow at the *École Poly-*

technique. Embrace me !" And the Emperor fell
upon my neck in the presence of his entire staff.
Then, recovering himself, he gently placed in my
hand his own magnificent snuff-box, in exchange
for mine, and hanging upon my breast the cross
of the Legion of Honor which he took from his
own, he bade one of his Marshals conduct me
back to my regiment.

I was so intoxicated with the honor of which I
had been the recipient, that on reaching our lines
I uttered a shout of joy and put spurs to my
horse. The intelligent animal seemed to sympathize with my feelings, and fairly flew over the
ground. On a rising eminence a few yards before
me stood a gray-haired officer, surrounded by his
staff. I don't know what possessed me, but putting spurs to my horse, I rode at him boldly, and
with one bound cleared him, horse and all. A
shout of indignation arose from the assembled
staff. I wheeled suddenly, with the intention of
apologizing, but my mare misunderstood me, and,
again dashing forward, once more vaulted over
the head of the officer, this time unfortunately
uncovering him by a vicious kick of her hoof.

"Seize him!" roared the entire army. I was seized. As the soldiers led me away, I asked the name of the gray-haired officer. "That — why, that 's the DUKE OF WELLINGTON!"

I fainted.

*   *   *   *   *   *

For six months I had brain-fever. During my illness ten grapeshot were extracted from my body which I had unconsciously received during the battle. When I opened my eyes I met the sweet glance of a Sister of Charity.

"Blanche!" I stammered feebly.

"The same," she replied.

"You here?"

"Yes, dear; but hush! It 's a long story. You see, dear Terence, your grandfather married my great-aunt's sister, and your father again married my grandmother's niece, who, dying without a will, was, according to the French law —"

"But I do not comprehend," I said.

"Of course not," said Blanche, with her old sweet smile; "you 've had brain-fever; so go to sleep."

I understood, however, that Blanche loved me; and I am now, dear reader, Sir Terence Sackville, K. C. B., and Lady Blanche is Lady Sackville.

SELINA SEDILIA.

By MISS M. E. B—DD—N AND MRS. H—N—Y W—D.

CHAPTER I.

THE sun was setting over Sloperton Grange, and reddened the window of the lonely chamber in the western tower, supposed to be haunted by Sir Edward Sedilia, the founder of the Grange. In the dreamy distance arose the gilded mausoleum of Lady Felicia Sedilia, who haunted that portion of Sedilia Manor, known as "Stiff-uns Acre." A little to the left of the Grange might have been seen a mouldering ruin, known as "Guy's Keep," haunted by the spirit of Sir Guy Sedilia, who was found, one morning, crushed by one of the fallen battlements. Yet, as the setting sun gilded these objects, a beautiful and almost holy calm seemed diffused about the Grange.

The Lady Selina sat by an oriel window, over-looking the park. The sun sank gently in the bosom of the German Ocean, and yet the lady did not lift her beautiful head from the finely curved arm and diminutive hand which supported it. When darkness finally shrouded the landscape she started, for the sound of horse-hoofs clattered over the stones of the avenue. She had scarcely risen before an aristocratic young man fell on his knees before her.

"My Selina!"

"Edgardo! You here?"

"Yes, dearest."

"And — you — you — have — seen nothing?" said the lady in an agitated voice and nervous manner, turning her face aside to conceal her emotion.

"Nothing — that is nothing of any account," said Edgardo. "I passed the ghost of your aunt in the park, noticed the spectre of your uncle in the ruined keep, and observed the familiar features of the spirit of your great-grandfather at his usual post. But nothing beyond these trifles, my Selina. Nothing more, love, absolutely nothing."

The young man turned his dark liquid orbs fondly upon the ingenuous face of his betrothed.

"My own Edgardo!— and you still love me? You still would marry me in spite of this dark mystery which surrounds me? In spite of the fatal history of my race? In spite of the ominous predictions of my aged nurse?"

"I would, Selina"; and the young man passed his arm around her yielding waist. The two lovers gazed at each other's faces in unspeakable bliss. Suddenly Selina started.

"Leave me, Edgardo! leave me! A mysterious something — a fatal misgiving — a dark ambiguity — an equivocal mistrust oppresses me. I would be alone!"

The young man arose, and cast a loving glance on the lady. "Then we will be married on the seventeenth."

"The seventeenth," repeated Selina, with a mysterious shudder.

They embraced and parted. As the clatter of hoofs in the court-yard died away, the Lady Selina sank into the chair she had just quitted.

"The seventeenth," she repeated slowly, with the same fateful shudder. "Ah!— what if he should know that I have another husband living?

Dare I reveal to him that I have two legitimate and three natural children ? Dare I repeat to him the history of my youth ? Dare I confess that at the age of seven I poisoned my sister, by putting verdigris in her cream-tarts, — that I threw my cousin from a swing at the age of twelve ? That the lady's-maid who incurred the displeasure of my girlhood now lies at the bottom of the horse-pond ? No ! no ! he is too pure, — too good, — too innocent, to hear such improper conversation !" and her whole body writhed as she rocked to and fro in a paroxysm of grief.

But she was soon calm. Rising to her feet, she opened a secret panel in the wall, and revealed a slow-match ready for lighting.

"This match," said the Lady Selina, "is connected with a mine beneath the western tower, where my three children are confined ; another branch of it lies under the parish church, where the record of my first marriage is kept. I have only to light this match and the whole of my past life is swept away !" She approached the match with a lighted candle.

But a hand was laid upon her arm, and with a

shriek the Lady Selina fell on her knees before the
spectre of Sir Guy.

CHAPTER II.

" FORBEAR, Selina," said the phantom in a hollow voice.

" Why should I forbear ? " responded Selina
haughtily, as she recovered her courage. " You
know the secret of our race ? "

" I do. Understand me, — I do not object to
the eccentricities of your youth. I know the fearful destiny which, pursuing you, led you to poison
your sister and drown your lady's-maid. I know
the awful doom which I have brought upon this
house ! But if you make way with these children — "

" Well," said the Lady Selina, hastily

" They will haunt you ! "

" Well, I fear them not," said Selina, drawing
her superb figure to its full height.

" Yes, but, my dear child, what place are they
to haunt ? The ruin is sacred to your uncle's

spirit. Your aunt monopolizes the park, and, I must be allowed to state, not unfrequently trespasses upon the grounds of others. The horsepond is frequented by the spirit of your maid, and your murdered sister walks these corridors. To be plain, there is no room at Sloperton Grange for another ghost. I cannot have them in my room, — for you know I don't like children. Think of this, rash girl, and forbear ! Would you, Selina," said the phantom, mournfully, — " would you force your great-grandfather's spirit to take lodgings elsewhere ? "

Lady Selina's hand trembled ; the lighted candle fell from her nerveless fingers.

" No," she cried passionately ; " never ! " and fell fainting to the floor.

CHAPTER III.

EDGARDO galloped rapidly towards Sloperton. When the outline of the Grange had faded away in the darkness, he reined his magnificent steed beside the ruins of Guy's Keep.

"It wants but a few minutes of the hour," he said, consulting his watch by the light of the moon. "He dare not break his word. He will come." He paused, and peered anxiously into the darkness. "But come what may, she is mine," he continued, as his thoughts reverted fondly to the fair lady he had quitted. "Yet if she knew all. If she knew that I were a disgraced and ruined man, — a felon and an outcast. If she knew that at the age of fourteen I murdered my Latin tutor and forged my uncle's will. If she knew that I had three wives already, and that the fourth victim of misplaced confidence and my unfortunate peculiarity is expected to be at Sloperton by to-night's train with her baby. But no ; she must not know it. Constance must not arrive. Burke the Slogger must attend to that.

"Ha! here he is! Well?"

These words were addressed to a ruffian in a slouched hat, who suddenly appeared from Guy's Keep.

"I be's here, measter," said the villain, with a disgracefully low accent and complete disregard of grammatical rules.

" It is well. Listen: I 'm in possession of facts that will send you to the gallows. I know of the murder of Bill Smithers, the robbery of the toll-gate-keeper, and the making away of the youngest daughter of Sir Reginald de Walton. A word from me, and the officers of justice are on your track."

Burke the Slogger trembled.

" Hark ye ! serve my purpose, and I may yet save you. The 5.30 train from Clapham will be due at Sloperton at 9.25. *It must not arrive !* "

The villain's eyes sparkled as he nodded at Edgardo.

" Enough, — you understand ; leave me ! "

CHAPTER IV.

ABOUT half a mile from Sloperton Station the South Clapham and Medway line crossed a bridge over Sloperton-on-Trent. As the shades of evening were closing, a man in a slouched hat might have been seen carrying a saw and axe under his arm, hanging about the bridge. From time to

time he disappeared in the shadow of its abut-
ments, but the sound of a saw and axe still betrayed his vicinity. At exactly nine o'clock he
reappeared, and, crossing to the Sloperton side,
rested his shoulder against the abutment and gave
a shove. The bridge swayed a moment, and then
fell with a splash into the water, leaving a space
of one hundred feet between the two banks. This
done, Burke the Slogger, — for it was he, — with a
fiendish chuckle seated himself on the divided
railway track and awaited the coming of the
train.

A shriek from the woods announced its approach. For an instant Burke the Slogger saw
the glaring of a red lamp. The ground trembled.
The train was going with fearful rapidity. Another second and it had reached the bank. Burke
the Slogger uttered a fiendish laugh. But the
next moment the train leaped across the chasm,
striking the rails exactly even, and, dashing out
the life of Burke the Slogger, sped away to
Sloperton.

The first object that greeted Edgardo, as he rode
up to the station on the arrival of the train, was

the body of Burke the Slogger hanging on the
cow-catcher; the second was the face of his deserted wife looking from the windows of a second-
class carriage.

CHAPTER V.

A NAMELESS terror seemed to have taken possession of Clarissa, Lady Selina's maid, as she
rushed into the presence of her mistress.

"O my lady, such news!"

"Explain yourself," said her mistress, rising.

"An accident has happened on the railway, and
a man has been killed."

"What — not Edgardo!" almost screamed Selina.

"No, Burke the Slogger!" your ladyship.

"My first husband!" said Lady Selina, sinking
on her knees. "Just Heaven, I thank thee!"

CHAPTER VI.

THE morning of the seventeenth dawned brightly over Sloperton. "A fine day for the wedding," said the sexton to Swipes, the butler of Sloperton Grange. The aged retainer shook his head sadly. "Alas! there's no trusting in signs!" he continued. "Seventy-five years ago, on a day like this, my young mistress —" But he was cut short by the appearance of a stranger.

"I would see Sir Edgardo," said the new-comer, impatiently.

The bridegroom, who, with the rest of the wedding-train, was about stepping into the carriage to proceed to the parish church, drew the stranger aside.

"It's done!" said the stranger, in a hoarse whisper.

"Ah! and you buried her?"

"With the others!"

"Enough. No more at present. Meet me after the ceremony, and you shall have your reward."

The stranger shuffled away, and Edgardo returned to his bride. " A trifling matter of business I had forgotten, my dear Selina ; let us proceed." And the young man pressed the timid hand of his blushing bride as he handed her into the carriage. The cavalcade rode out of the court-yard. At the same moment, the deep bell on Guy's Keep tolled ominously.

CHAPTER VII.

SCARCELY had the wedding-train left the Grange, than Alice Sedilia, youngest daughter of Lady Selina, made her escape from the western tower, owing to a lack of watchfulness on the part of Clarissa. The innocent child, freed from restraint, rambled through the lonely corridors, and finally, opening a door, found herself in her mother's boudoir. For some time she amused herself by examining the various ornaments and elegant trifles with which it was filled. Then, in pursuance of a childish freak, she dressed herself in her mother's laces and ribbons. In this occupation she chanced to touch a peg which proved to be a spring that opened a secret panel in the wall. Alice uttered a cry of delight as she noticed what, to her childish fancy, appeared to be the slow-match of a fire-work. Taking a lucifer match in her hand she approached the fuse. She hesitated a moment. What would her mother and her nurse say?

Suddenly the ringing of the chimes of Sloperton parish church met her ear. Alice knew that the sound signified that the marriage party had entered the church, and that she was secure from interruption. With a childish smile upon her lips, Alice Sedilia touched off the slow-match.

CHAPTER VIII.

AT exactly two o'clock on the seventeenth, Rupert Sedilia, who had just returned from India, was thoughtfully descending the hill toward Sloperton manor. "If I can prove that my aunt Lady Selina was married before my father died,

I can establish my claim to Sloperton Grange,"
he uttered, half aloud. He paused, for a sudden
trembling of the earth beneath his feet, and a
terrific explosion, as of a park of artillery, arrested
his progress. At the same moment he beheld a
dense cloud of smoke envelop the churchyard
of Sloperton, and the western tower of the Grange
seemed to be lifted bodily from its foundation.
The air seemed filled with falling fragments, and
two dark objects struck the earth close at his feet.
Rupert picked them up. One seemed to be a
heavy volume bound in brass.

A cry burst from his lips.

" The Parish Records." He opened the volume
hastily. It contained the marriage of Lady Selina
to " Burke the Slogger."

The second object proved to be a piece of parch-
ment. He tore it open with trembling fingers. It
was the missing will of Sir James Sedilia !

CHAPTER IX.

WHEN the bells again rang on the new parish church of Sloperton it was for the marriage of Sir Rupert Sedilia and his cousin, the only remaining members of the family.

Five more ghosts were added to the supernatural population of Sloperton Grange. Perhaps this was the reason why Sir Rupert sold the property shortly afterward, and that for many years a dark shadow seemed to hang over the ruins of Sloperton Grange.

THE NINETY-NINE GUARDSMEN.

By AL—X—D—R D—M—S.

CHAPTER I.

SHOWING THE QUALITY OF THE CUSTOMERS OF THE INN-KEEPER OF PROVINS.

TWENTY years after, the gigantic innkeeper of Provins stood looking at a cloud of dust on the highway.

This cloud of dust betokened the approach of a traveller. Travellers had been rare that season on the highway between Paris and Provins.

The heart of the innkeeper rejoiced. Turning to Dame Perigord, his wife, he said, stroking his white apron : —

" St. Denis ! make haste and spread the cloth. Add a bottle of Charlevoix to the table. This traveller, who rides so fast, by his pace must be a Monseigneur."

Truly the traveller, clad in the uniform of a

musketeer, as he drew up to the door of the hostelry, did not seem to have spared his horse. Throwing his reins to the landlord, he leaped lightly to the ground. He was a young man of four-and-twenty, and spoke with a slight Gascon accent.

"I am hungry, *Morbleu !* I wish to dine !"

The gigantic innkeeper bowed and led the way to a neat apartment, where a table stood covered with tempting viands. The musketeer at once set to work. Fowls, fish, and *pâtés* disappeared before him. Perigord sighed as he witnessed the devastations. Only once the stranger paused.

"Wine !" Perigord brought wine. The stranger drank a dozen bottles. Finally he rose to depart. Turning to the expectant landlord, he said : —

"Charge it."

"To whom, your highness ?" said Perigord, anxiously.

"To his Eminence !"

"Mazarin !" ejaculated the innkeeper.

"The same. Bring me my horse," and the musketeer, remounting his favorite animal, rode away.

The innkeeper slowly turned back into the inn

Scarcely had he reached the courtyard before the clatter of hoofs again called him to the doorway. A young musketeer of a light and graceful figure rode up.

"*Parbleu*, my dear Perigord, I am famishing. What have you got for dinner?"

"Venison, capons, larks, and pigeons, your excellency," replied the obsequious landlord, bowing to the ground.

"Enough!" The young musketeer dismounted and entered the inn. Seating himself at the table replenished by the careful Perigord, he speedily swept it as clean as the first comer.

"Some wine, my brave Perigord," said the graceful young musketeer, as soon as he could find utterance.

Perigord brought three dozen of Charlevoix. The young man emptied them almost at a draught.

"By-by, Perigord," he said lightly, waving his hand, as, preceding the astonished landlord, he slowly withdrew.

"But, your highness,— the bill," said the astounded Perigord.

"Ah, the bill. Charge it!"

" To whom ? "

" The Queen ! "

" What, Madame ? "

" The same. Adieu, my good Perigord." And the graceful stranger rode away. An interval of quiet succeeded, in which the innkeeper gazed wofully at his wife. Suddenly he was startled by a clatter of hoofs, and an aristocratic figure stood in the doorway.

"Ah," said the courtier good-naturedly. "What, do my eyes deceive me ? No, it is the festive and luxurious Perigord. Perigord, listen. I famish. I languish. I would dine."

The innkeeper again covered the table with viands. Again it was swept clean as the fields of Egypt before the miraculous swarm of locusts. The stranger looked up.

" Bring me another fowl, my Perigord."

" Impossible, your excellency ; the larder is stripped clean."

" Another flitch of bacon, then."

" Impossible, your highness ; there is no more."

" Well, then, wine ! "

The landlord brought one hundred and forty-four bottles. The courtier drank them all.

"One may drink if one cannot eat," said the aristocratic stranger, good-humoredly.

The innkeeper shuddered.

The guest rose to depart. The innkeeper came slowly forward with his bill, to which he had covertly added the losses which he had suffered from the previous strangers.

"Ah, the bill. Charge it."

"Charge it! to whom?"

"To the King," said the guest.

"What! his Majesty?"

"Certainly. Farewell, Perigord."

The innkeeper groaned. Then he went out and took down his sign. Then remarked to his wife: —

"I am a plain man, and don't understand politics. It seems, however, that the country is in a troubled state. Between his Eminence the Cardinal, his Majesty the King, and her Majesty the Queen, I am a ruined man."

"Stay," said Dame Perigord, "I have an idea."

"And that is — "

"Become yourself a musketeer."

CHAPTER II.

THE COMBAT.

ON leaving Provins the first musketeer proceeded to Nangis, where he was reinforced by thirty-three followers. The second musketeer, arriving at Nangis at the same moment, placed himself at the head of thirty-three more. The third guest of the landlord of Provins arrived at Nangis in time to assemble together thirty-three other musketeers.

The first stranger led the troops of his Eminence.

The second led the troops of the Queen.

The third led the troops of the King.

The fight commenced. It raged terribly for seven hours. The first musketeer killed thirty of the Queen's troops. The second musketeer killed thirty of the King's troops. The third musketeer killed thirty of his Eminence's troops.

By this time it will be perceived the number of

musketeers had been narrowed down to four on each side.

Naturally the three principal warriors approached each other.

They simultaneously uttered a cry.

" Aramis ! "

" Athos ! "

" D'Artagnan ! "

They fell into each other's arms.

" And it seems that we are fighting against each other, my children," said the Count de la Fere, mournfully.

" How singular ! " exclaimed Aramis and D'Artagnan.

" Let us stop this fratricidal warfare," said Athos.

" We will ! " they exclaimed together.

" But how to disband our followers ? " queried D'Artagnan.

Aramis winked. They understood each other. " Let us cut 'em down ! "

They cut 'em down. Aramis killed three. D'Artagnan three. Athos three.

The friends again embraced. " How like old times," said Aramis. " How touching ! " exclaimed the serious and philosophic Count de la Fere.

The galloping of hoofs caused them to withdraw from each other's embraces. A gigantic figure rapidly approached.

"The innkeeper of Provins !" they cried, drawing their swords.

"Perigord, down with him !" shouted D'Artagnan.

"Stay," said Athos.

The gigantic figure was beside them. He uttered a cry.

"Athos, Aramis, D'Artagnan !"

"Porthos !" exclaimed the astonished trio.

"The same." They all fell in each other's arms.

The Count de la Fere slowly raised his hands to Heaven. "Bless you ! Bless us, my children ! However different our opinion may be in regard to politics, we have but one opinion in regard to our own merits. Where can you find a better man than Aramus ?"

"Than Porthos ?" said Aramis.

"Than D'Artagnan ?" said Porthos.

"Than Athos ?" said D'Artagnan.

CHAPTER III.

SHOWING HOW THE KING OF FRANCE WENT UP A LADDER.

THE King descended into the garden. Proceeding cautiously along the terraced walk, he came to the wall immediately below the windows of Madame. To the left were two windows, concealed by vines. They opened into the apartments of La Valliere.

The King sighed.

"It is about nineteen feet to that window," said the King. "If I had a ladder about nineteen feet long, it would reach to that window. This is logic."

Suddenly the King stumbled over something. "St. Denis!" he exclaimed, looking down. It was a ladder, just nineteen feet long.

The King placed it against the wall. In so doing, he fixed the lower end upon the abdomen of a man who lay concealed by the wall. The man did not utter a cry or wince. The King suspected nothing. He ascended the ladder.

The ladder was too short. Louis the Grand was not a tall man. He was still two feet below the window.

"Dear me!" said the King.

Suddenly the ladder was lifted two feet from below. This enabled the King to leap in the window. At the farther end of the apartment stood a young girl, with red hair and a lame leg. She was trembling with emotion.

"Louise!"

"The King!"

"Ah, my God, mademoiselle."

"Ah, my God, sire."

But a low knock at the door interrupted the lovers. The King uttered a cry of rage; Louise one of despair.

The door opened and D'Artagnan entered.

"Good evening, sire," said the musketeer.

The King touched a bell. Porthos appeared in the doorway.

"Good evening, sire."

"Arrest M. D'Artagnan."

Porthos looked at D'Artagnan, and did not move.

The King almost turned purple with rage.   He
again touched the bell.   Athos entered.

" Count, arrest Porthos and D'Artagnan."

The Count de la Fere glanced at Porthos and
D'Artagnan, and smiled sweetly.

" *Sacre !*   Where is Aramis ? " said the King,
violently.

" Here, sire," and Aramis entered.

" Arrest Athos, Porthos, and D'Artagnan."

Aramis bowed and folded his arms.

" Arrest yourself ! "

Aramis did not move.

The King shuddered and turned pale.   " Am I
not King of France ? "

" Assuredly, sire, but we are also severally, Porthos, Aramis, D'Artagnan, and Athos."

" Ah ! " said the King.

" Yes, sire."

" What does this mean ? "

" It means, your Majesty," said Aramis, stepping
forward, " that your conduct as a married man is
highly improper.   I am an Abbé, and I object to
these improprieties.   My friends here, D'Artagnan,
Athos, and Porthos, pure-minded young men, are

also terribly shocked. Observe, sire, how they blush!"

Athos, Porthos, and D'Artagnan blushed.

"Ah," said the King, thoughtfully. "You teach me a lesson. You are devoted and noble young gentlemen, but your only weakness is your excessive modesty. From this moment I make you all Marshals and Dukes, with the exception of Aramis.

"And me, sire?" said Aramis.

"You shall be an Archbishop!"

The four friends looked up and then rushed into each other's arms. The King embraced Louise de la Valliere, by way of keeping them company. A pause ensued. At last Athos spoke: —

"Swear, my children, that, next to yourselves, you will. respect — the King of France; and remember that 'Forty years after' we will meet again."

THE DWELLER OF THE THRESHOLD.

By SIR ED—D L—TT—N B—LW—R.

BOOK I.

THE PROMPTINGS OF THE IDEAL.

It was noon. Sir Edward had stepped from his brougham and was proceeding on foot down the Strand. He was dressed with his usual faultless taste, but in alighting from his vehicle his foot had slipped, and a small round disk of conglomerated soil, which instantly appeared on his high arched instep, marred the harmonious glitter of his boots. Sir Edward was fastidious. Casting his eyes around, at a little distance he perceived the stand of a youthful bootblack. Thither he sauntered, and carelessly placing his foot on the low stool, he waited the application of the polisher's art. "'T is true," said Sir Edward to himself, yet half aloud, "the contact of the Foul and the Disgusting mars the general effect of the Shiny and the Beautiful — and, yet, why am I here ? I repeat it, calmly and deliberately — why am I here ? Ha ! Boy !"

The Boy looked up — his dark Italian eyes glanced intelligently at the Philosopher, and as with one hand he tossed back his glossy curls from his marble brow, and with the other he spread the equally glossy Day & Martin over the Baronet's boot, he answered in deep rich tones: " The Ideal is subjective to the Real. The exercise of apperception gives a distinctiveness to idiocracy, which is, however, subject to the limits of ME. You are an admirer of the Beautiful, sir. You wish your boots blacked. The Beautiful is attainable by means of the Coin."

" Ah," said Sir Edward thoughtfully, gazing upon the almost supernal beauty of the Child before him ; " you speak well. You have read *Kant.*"

The Boy blushed deeply. He drew a copy of *Kant* from his blouse, but in his confusion several other volumes dropped from his bosom on the ground. The Baronet picked them up.

" Ah !" said the Philosopher, " what 's this ?

Cicero's De Senectute, at your age, too ?   *Martial's Epigrams, Cæsar's Commentaries.*   What ! a classical scholar ? "

" E pluribus Unum.   Nux vomica.   Nil desperandum.   Nihil fit ! " said the Boy, enthusiastically. The Philosopher gazed at the Child.   A strange presence seemed to transfuse and possess him. Over the brow of the Boy glittered the pale nimbus of the Student.

" Ah, and Schiller's *Robbers,* too ? " queried the Philosopher.

" Das ist ausgespielt," said the Boy, modestly.

" Then you have read my translation of *Schiller's Ballads ?* " continued the Baronet, with some show of interest.

" I have, and infinitely prefer them to the original," said the Boy, with intellectual warmth. " You have shown how in Actual life we strive for a Goal we cannot reach ; how in the Ideal the Goal is attainable, and there effort is victory.   You have given us the Antithesis which is a key to the Remainder, and constantly balances before us the conditions of the Actual and the privileges of the Ideal."

"My very words," said the Baronet; "wonder-ful, wonderful!" and he gazed fondly at the Italian boy, who again resumed his menial employment. Alas! the wings of the Ideal were folded. The Student had been absorbed in the Boy.

But Sir Edward's boots were blacked, and he turned to depart. Placing his hand upon the clustering tendrils that surrounded the classic nob of the infant Italian, he said softly, like a strain of distant music : —

"Boy, you have done well. Love the Good. Protect the Innocent. Provide for The Indigent. Respect the Philosopher. . . . . Stay! Can you tell we what *is* The True, The Beautiful, The In-nocent, The Virtuous?"

"They are things that commence with a capital letter," said the Boy, promptly.

"Enough! Respect everything that commences with a capital letter! Respect ME!" and drop-ping a half-penny in the hand of the boy, he departed.

The Boy gazed fixedly at the coin. A frightful and instantaneous change overspread his features. His noble brow was corrugated with baser lines of calculation. His black eye, serpent-like, glittered with suppressed passion. Dropping upon his hands and feet, he crawled to the curbstone and hissed after the retreating form of the Baronet, the single word: —

"Bilk!"

BOOK II.

IN THE WORLD.

"ELEVEN years ago," said Sir Edward to himself, as his brougham slowly rolled him toward the Committee Room; "just eleven years ago my natural son disappeared mysteriously. I have no doubt in the world but that this little bootblack is he. His mother died in Italy. He resembles his mother very much. Perhaps I ought to provide for him. Shall I disclose myself? No! no! Better he should taste the sweets of Labor. Penury ennobles the mind and kindles the Love of the Beautiful. I will act to him, not like a Father, not like a Guardian, not like a Friend — but like a Philosopher!"

With these words, Sir Edward entered the Committee Room. His Secretary approached him. "Sir Edward, there are fears of a division in the House, and the Prime Minister has sent for you."

"I will be there," said Sir Edward, as he placed his hand on his chest and uttered a hollow cough!

No one who heard the Baronet that night, in his sarcastic and withering speech on the Drainage and Sewerage Bill, would have recognized the lover of the Ideal and the Philosopher of the Beautiful. No one who listened to his eloquence would have dreamed of the Spartan resolution this iron man had taken in regard to the Lost Boy — his own beloved Lionel. None!

"A fine speech from Sir Edward to-night," said Lord Billingsgate, as, arm-and-arm with the Premier, he entered his carriage.

"Yes! but how dreadfully he coughs!"

"Exactly. Dr. Bolus says his lungs are entirely gone; he breathes entirely by an effort of will, and altogether independent of pulmonary assistance."

"How strange!" and the carriage rolled away.

BOOK III.

THE DWELLER OF THE THRESHOLD.

"ADON AI, appear! appear!"

And as the Seer spoke, the awful Presence glided out of Nothingness, and sat, sphinx-like, at the feet of the Alchemist.

"I am come!" said the Thing.

"You should say, 'I have come,' — it's better grammar," said the Boy-Neophyte, thoughtfully accenting the substituted expression.

"Hush, rash Boy," said the Seer, sternly. "Would you oppose your feeble knowledge to the infinite intelligence of the Unmistakable? A word, and you are lost forever."

The Boy breathed a silent prayer, and, handing a sealed package to the Seer, begged him to hand it to his father in case of his premature decease.

"You have sent for me," hissed the Presence. "Behold me, Apokatharticon, — the Unpronounceable. In me all things exist that are not already coexistent.   I am the Unattainable, the Intangible, the Cause, and the Effect.   In me observe the Brahma of Mr. Emerson ; not only Brahma himself, but also the sacred musical composition rehearsed by the faithful Hindoo.   I am the real Gyges.   None others are genuine."

And the veiled Son of the Starbeam laid himself loosely about the room, and permeated Space generally.

" Unfathomable Mystery," said the Rosicrucian in a low, sweet voice. " Brave Child with the Vitreous Optic !   Thou who pervadest all things and rubbest against us without abrasion of the cuticle. I command thee, speak ! "

And the misty, intangible, indefinite Presence spoke.

BOOK IV.

MYSELF.

AFTER the events related in the last chapter, the reader will perceive that nothing was easier than to reconcile Sir Edward to his son Lionel, nor to resuscitate the beautiful Italian girl, who, it ap-

pears, was not dead, and to cause Sir Edward to
marry his first and boyish love, whom he had deserted. They were married in St. George's, Han -
over Square. As the bridal party stood before the
altar, Sir Edward, with a sweet sad smile, said, in
quite his old manner: —

"The Sublime and Beautiful are the Real; the
only Ideal is the Ridiculous and Homely. Let us
always remember this. Let us through life endeavor to personify the virtues, and always begin
'em with a capital letter. Let us, whenever we
can find an opportunity, deliver our sentiments in
the form of round-hand copies. Respect the Aged.
Eschew Vulgarity. Admire Ourselves. Regard
the Novelist."

THE HAUNTED MAN.

A CHRISTMAS STORY.

By CH—R—S D—CK—N—S.

——◆——

PART I.

THE FIRST PHANTOM.

Don't tell me that it was n't a knocker. I had
seen it often enough, and I ought to know. So
ought the three-o'clock beer, in dirty high-lows,
swinging himself over the railing, or executing a
demoniacal jig upon the doorstep; so ought the
butcher, although butchers as a general thing are
scornful of such trifles; so ought the postman, to
whom knockers of the most extravagant descrip-
tion were merely human weaknesses, that were to
be pitied and used. And so ought, for the matter
of that, etc., etc., etc.

But then it was *such* a knocker. A wild, ex-
travagant, and utterly incomprehensible knocker.
A knocker so mysterious and suspicious that
Policeman X 37, first coming upon it, felt inclined

to take it instantly in custody, but compromised with his professional instincts by sharply and sternly noting it with an eye that admitted of no nonsense, but confidently expected to detect its secret yet. An ugly knocker; a knocker with a hard, human face, that was a type of the harder human face within. A human face that held between its teeth a brazen rod. So hereafter, in the mysterious future should be held, etc., etc.

But if the knocker had a fierce human aspect in the glare of day, you should have seen it at night, when it peered out of the gathering shadows and suggested an ambushed figure; when the light of the street lamps fell upon it, and wrought a play of sinister expression in its hard outlines; when it seemed to wink meaningly at a shrouded figure who, as the night fell darkly, crept up the steps and passed into the mysterious house; when the swinging door disclosed a black passage into which the figure seemed to lose itself and become a part of the mysterious gloom; when the night grew boisterous and the fierce wind made furious charges at the knocker, as if to wrench it off and carry it away in triumph. Such a night as this.

It was a wild and pitiless wind. A wind that had commenced life as a gentle country zephyr, but wandering through manufacturing towns had become demoralized, and reaching the city had plunged into extravagant dissipation and wild excesses. A roistering wind that indulged in Bacchanalian shouts on the street corners, that knocked off the hats from the heads of helpless passengers, and then fulfilled its duties by speeding away, like all young prodigals, — to sea.

He sat alone in a gloomy library listening to the wind that roared in the chimney. Around him novels and story-books were strewn thickly; in his lap he held one with its pages freshly cut, and turned the leaves wearily until his eyes rested upon a portrait in its frontispiece. And as the wind howled the more fiercely, and the darkness without fell blacker, a strange and fateful likeness to that portrait appeared above his chair and leaned upon his shoulder. The Haunted Man gazed at the portrait and sighed. The figure gazed at the portrait and sighed too.

" Here again ? " said the Haunted Man.

" Here again," it repeated in a low voice.

4—V. 5

" Another novel ? "

" Another novel."

" The old story ? "

" The old story."

" I see a child," said the Haunted Man, gazing from the pages of the book into the fire, — " a most unnatural child, a model infant. It is prematurely old and philosophic. It dies in poverty to slow music. It dies surrounded by luxury to slow music. It dies with an accompaniment of golden water and rattling carts to slow music. Previous to its decease it makes a will ; it repeats the Lord's Prayer, it kisses the 'boofer lady.' That child — "

" Is mine," said the phantom.

" I see a good woman, undersized. I see several charming women, but they are all undersized. They are more or less imbecile and idiotic, but always fascinating and undersized. They wear coquettish caps and aprons. I observe that feminine virtue is invariably below the medium height, and that it is always simple and infantine. These women — "

" Are mine."

" I see a haughty, proud, and wicked lady. She

is tall and queenly. I remark that all proud and wicked women are tall and queenly. That woman — "

" Is mine," said the phantom, wringing his hands.

" I see several things continually impending. I observe that whenever an accident, a murder, or death is about to happen, there is something in the furniture, in the locality, in the atmosphere, that foreshadows and suggests it years in advance. I cannot say that in real life I have noticed it, — the perception of this surprising fact belongs — "

" To me ! " said the phantom. The Haunted Man continued, in a despairing tone : —

" I see the influence of this in the magazines and daily papers ; I see weak imitators rise up and enfeeble the world with senseless formula. I am getting tired of it. It won't do, Charles ! it won't do ! " and the Haunted Man buried his head in his hands and groaned. The figure looked down upon him sternly : the portrait in the frontispiece frowned as he gazed.

" Wretched man," said the phantom, " and how have these things affected you ? "

"Once I laughed and cried, but then I was younger. Now, I would forget them if I could."

"Have then your wish. And take this with you, man whom I renounce. From this day henceforth you shall live with those whom I displace. Without forgetting me, 't will be your lot to walk through life as if we had not met. But first you shall survey these scenes that henceforth must be yours. At one to-night, prepare to meet the phantom I have raised. Farewell!"

The sound of its voice seemed to fade away with the dying wind, and the Haunted Man was alone. But the firelight flickered gayly, and the light danced on the walls, making grotesque figures of the furniture.

"Ha, ha!" said the Haunted Man, rubbing his hands gleefully; "now for a whiskey punch and a cigar."

BOOK II.

THE SECOND PHANTOM.

ONE ! The stroke of the far-off bell had hardly died before the front door closed with a reverberating clang. Steps were heard along the passage ; the library door swung open of itself, and the Knocker — yes, the Knocker — slowly strode into the room. The Haunted Man rubbed his eyes, — no ! there could be no mistake about it, — it was the Knocker's face, mounted on a misty, almost imperceptible body. The brazen rod was transferred from its mouth to its right hand, where it was held like a ghostly truncheon.

" It 's a cold evening," said the Haunted Man.

" It is," said the Goblin, in a hard, metallic voice.

" It must be pretty cold out there," said the Haunted Man, with vague politeness. " Do you ever — will you — take some hot water and brandy ? "

" No," said the Goblin.

"Perhaps you'd like it cold, by way of change?" continued the Haunted Man, correcting himself, as he remembered the peculiar temperature with which the Goblin was probably familiar.

"Time flies," said the Goblin coldly. "We have no leisure for idle talk. Come!" He moved his ghostly truncheon toward the window, and laid his hand upon the other's arm. At his touch the body of the Haunted Man seemed to become as thin and incorporeal as that of the Goblin himself, and together they glided out of the window into the black and blowy night.

In the rapidity of their flight the senses of the Haunted Man seemed to leave him. At length they stopped suddenly.

"What do you see?" asked the Goblin.

"I see a battlemented mediæval castle. Gallant men in mail ride over the drawbridge, and kiss their gauntleted fingers to fair ladies, who wave their lily hands in return. I see fight and fray and tournament. I hear roaring heralds bawling the charms of delicate women, and shamelessly proclaiming their lovers. Stay. I see a Jewess about to leap from a battlement. I see knightly

deeds, violence, rapine, and a good deal of blood.
I 've seen pretty much the same at Astley's."

" Look again."

" I see purple moors, glens, masculine women,
bare-legged men, priggish book-worms, more violence, physical excellence, and blood. Always
blood, — and the superiority of physical attain-
ments."

" And how do you feel now ? " said the Goblin.

The Haunted Man shrugged his shoulders.
" None the better for being carried back and
asked to sympathize with a barbarous age."

The Goblin smiled and clutched his arm ; they
again sped rapidly through the black night and
again halted.

" What do you see ? " said the Goblin.

" I see a barrack room, with a mess table, and a
group of intoxicated Celtic officers telling funny
stories, and giving challenges to duel. I see a
young Irish gentleman capable of performing
prodigies of valor. I learn incidentally that the
acme of all heroism is the cornetcy of a dragoon
regiment. I hear a good deal of French ! No,
thank you," said the Haunted Man hurriedly, as

he stayed the waving hand of the Goblin; "I would rather *not* go to the Peninsula, and don't care to have a private interview with Napoleon."

Again the Goblin flew away with the unfortunate man, and from a strange roaring below them he judged they were above the ocean. A ship hove in sight, and the Goblin stayed its flight. "Look," he said, squeezing his companion's arm.

The Haunted Man yawned. "Don't you think, Charles, you're rather running this thing into the ground? Of course it's very moral and instructive, and all that. But ain't there a little too much pantomime about it? Come now!"

"Look!" repeated the Goblin, pinching his arm malevolently. The Haunted Man groaned.

"O, of course, I see her Majesty's ship Arethusa. Of course I am familiar with her stern First Lieutenant, her eccentric Captain, her one fascinating and several mischievous midshipmen. Of course I know it's a splendid thing to see all this, and not to be seasick. O, there the young gentlemen are going to play a trick on the purser.

For God's sake, let us go," and the unhappy man absolutely dragged the Goblin away with him.

When they next halted, it was at the edge of a broad and boundless prairie, in the middle of an oak opening.

"I see," said the Haunted Man, without waiting for his cue, but mechanically, and as if he were repeating a lesson which the Goblin had taught him, — "I see the Noble Savage. He is very fine to look at! But I observe under his war-paint, feathers, and picturesque blanket, dirt, disease, and an unsymmetrical contour. I observe beneath his inflated rhetoric deceit and hypocrisy; beneath his physical hardihood, cruelty, malice, and revenge. The Noble Savage is a humbug. I remarked the same to Mr. Catlin."

"Come," said the phantom.

The Haunted Man sighed, and took out his watch. "Could n't we do the rest of this another time?"

"My hour is almost spent, irreverent being, but there is yet a chance for your reformation. Come!"

Again they sped through the night, and again

halted. The sound of delicious but melancholy music fell upon their ears.

"I see," said the Haunted Man, with something of interest in his manner, — "I see an old moss-covered manse beside a sluggish, flowing river. I see weird shapes : witches, Puritans, clergymen, little children, judges, mesmerized maidens, moving to the sound of melody that thrills me with its sweetness and purity. But, although carried along its calm and evenly flowing current, the shapes are strange and frightful : an eating lichen gnaws at the heart of each. Not only the clergymen, but witch, maiden, judge, and Puritan, all wear Scarlet Letters of some kind burned upon their hearts. I am fascinated and thrilled, but I feel a morbid sensitiveness creeping over me. I — I beg your pardon." The Goblin was yawning frightfully. "Well, perhaps we had better go."

"One more, and the last," said the Goblin.

They were moving home. Streaks of red were beginning to appear in the eastern sky. Along the banks of the blackly flowing river by moorland and stagnant fens, by low houses, clustering close to the water's edge, like strange mollusks, crawled upon the beach to dry; by misty black barges, the more misty and indistinct seen through its mysterious veil, the river fog was slowly rising. So rolled away and rose from the heart of the Haunted Man, etc., etc.

They stopped before a quaint mansion of red brick. The Goblin waved his hand without speaking.

"I see," said the Haunted Man, "a gay drawing-room. I see my old friends of the club, of the college, of society, even as they lived and moved. I see the gallant and unselfish men, whom I have loved, and the snobs whom I have hated. I see strangely mingling with them, and now and then blending with their forms, our old friends Dick Steele, Addison, and Congreve. I observe, though, that these gentlemen have a habit of getting too much in the way. The royal standard of Queen Anne, not in itself a beautiful ornament, is rather too prominent in the picture. The long galleries of black oak, the formal furniture, the old portraits, are picturesque, but depressing. The house is damp. I enjoy myself better here on the lawn, where they are getting up a Vanity Fair. See, the bell rings, the curtain is rising, the puppets are brought out for a new play. Let me see."

The Haunted Man was pressing forward in his eagerness, but the hand of the Goblin stayed him, and pointing to his feet he saw, between him and the rising curtain, a new-made grave. And bending above the grave in passionate grief, the Haunted Man beheld the phantom of the previous night

*   *   *   *   *

The Haunted Man started, and — woke. The bright sunshine streamed into the room. The air was sparkling with frost. He ran joyously to the window and opened it. A small boy saluted him with " Merry Christmas." The Haunted Man instantly gave him a Bank of England note. " How much like Tiny Tim, Tom, and Bobby that boy looked, — bless my soul, what a genius this Dickens has ! "

A knock at the door, and Boots entered.

" Consider your salary doubled instantly. Have you read *David Copperfield ?* "

" Yezzur."

" Your salary is quadrupled. What do you think of the *Old Curiosity Shop ?* "

The man instantly burst into a torrent of tears, and then into a roar of laughter.

" Enough ! Here are five thousand pounds. Open a porter-house, and call it, ' Our Mutual Friend.' Huzza ! I feel so happy !" And the Haunted Man danced about the room.

And so, bathed in the light of that blessed sun, and yet glowing with the warmth of a good action, the Haunted Man, haunted no longer, save by those shapes which make the dreams of children beautiful, reseated himself in his chair, and finished *Our Mutual Friend.*

MISS MIX.

By CH—L—TTE BR—NTE.

CHAPEER I.

My earliest impressions are of a huge, mis-
shapen rock, against which the hoarse waves
beat unceasingly. On this rock three pelicans
are standing in a defiant attitude. A dark sky
lowers in the background, while two sea-gulls
and a gigantic cormorant eye with extreme dis-
favor the floating corpse of a drowned woman in
the foreground. A few bracelets, coral necklaces,
and other articles of jewelry, scattered around
loosely, complete this remarkable picture.

It is one which, in some vague, unconscious
way, symbolizes, to my fancy, the character of a
man. I have never been able to explain exactly
why. I think I must have seen the picture in
some illustrated volume, when a baby, or my
mother may have dreamed it before I was born.

As a child I was not handsome. When I consulted the triangular bit of looking-glass which I always carried with me, it showed a pale, sandy, and freckled face, shaded by locks like the color of seaweed when the sun strikes it in deep water. My eyes were said to be indistinctive; they were a faint, ashen gray; but above them rose — my only beauty — a high, massive, domelike forehead, with polished temples, like door-knobs of the purest porcelain.

Our family was a family of governesses. My mother had been one, and my sisters had the same occupation. Consequently, when, at the age of thirteen, my eldest sister handed me the advertisement of Mr. Rawjester, clipped from that day's "Times," I accepted it as my destiny. Nevertheless, a mysterious presentiment of an indefinite future haunted me in my dreams that night, as I lay upon my little snow-white bed. The next morning, with two bandboxes tied up in silk handkerchiefs, and a hair trunk, I turned my back upon Minerva Cottage forever.

CHAPTER II.

BLUNDERBORE HALL, the seat of James Rawjester, Esq., was encompassed by dark pines and
funereal hemlocks on all sides. The wind sang
weirdly in the turrets and moaned through the
long-drawn avenues of the park. As I approached
the house I saw several mysterious figures flit before the windows, and a yell of demoniac laughter
answered my summons at the bell. While I
strove to repress my gloomy forebodings, the
housekeeper, a timid, scared-looking old woman,
showed me into the library.

I entered, overcome with conflicting emotions.
I was dressed in a narrow gown of dark serge,
trimmed with black bugles. A thick green shawl
was pinned across my breast. My hands were
encased with black half-mittens worked with steel
beads; on my feet were large pattens, originally
the property of my deceased grandmother. I
carried a blue cotton umbrella. As I passed
before a mirror, I could not help glancing at it,

nor could I disguise from myself the fact that
I was not handsome.

Drawing a chair into a recess, I sat down with
folded hands, calmly awaiting the arrival of my
master. Once or twice a fearful yell rang through
the house, or the rattling of chains, and curses
uttered in a deep, manly voice, broke upon the
oppressive stillness. I began to feel my soul
rising with the emergency of the moment.

"You look alarmed, miss. You don't hear anything, my dear, do you?" asked the housekeeper
nervously.

"Nothing whatever," I remarked calmly, as a
terrific scream, followed by the dragging of chairs
and tables in the room above, drowned for a
moment my reply. "It is the silence, on the contrary, which has made me foolishly nervous."

The housekeeper looked at me approvingly, and
instantly made some tea for me.

I drank seven cups; as I was beginning the
eighth, I heard a crash, and the next moment a
man leaped into the room through the broken
window.

CHAPTER III.

THE crash startled me from my self-control. The housekeeper bent toward me and whispered : —

"Don't be excited. It 's Mr. Rawjester, — he prefers to come in sometimes in this way. It 's his playfulness, ha ! ha ! ha !"

"I perceive," I said calmly. "It 's the unfettered impulse of a lofty soul breaking the tyrannizing bonds of custom." And I turned toward him.

He had never once looked at me. He stood with his back to the fire, which set off the herculean breadth of his shoulders. His face was dark and expressive ; his under jaw squarely formed, and remarkably heavy. I was struck with his remarkable likeness to a Gorilla.

As he absently tied the poker into hard knots with his nervous fingers, I watched him with some interest. Suddenly he turned toward me : —

"Do you think I 'm handsome, young woman ?"

"Not classically beautiful," I returned calmly ; "but you have, if I may so express myself, an abstract manliness, — a sincere and wholesome barbarity which, involving as it does the naturalness —" But I stopped, for he yawned at that moment, — an action which singularly developed the immense breadth of his lower jaw, — and I saw he had forgotten me. Presently he turned to the housekeeper : —

"Leave us."

The old woman withdrew with a courtesy.

Mr. Rawjester deliberately turned his back upon me and remained silent for twenty minutes. I drew my shawl the more closely around my shoulders and closed my eyes.

"You are the governess ?" at length he said.

"I am, sir."

"A creature who teaches geography, arithmetic, and the use of the globes — ha ! — a wretched remnant of femininity, — a skimp pattern of girlhood with a premature flavor of tea-leaves and morality. Ugh !"

I bowed my head silently.

"Listen to me, girl !" he said sternly ; "this child you have come to teach — my ward — is not legitimate. She is the offspring of my mistress, — a common harlot. Ah! Miss Mix, what do you think of me now?"

"I admire," I replied calmly, "your sincerity. A mawkish regard for delicacy might have kept this disclosure to yourself. I only recognize in your frankness that perfect community of thought and sentiment which should exist between original natures."

I looked up; he had already forgotten my presence, and was engaged in pulling off his boots and coat. This done, he sank down in an arm-chair before the fire, and ran the poker wearily through his hair. I could not help pitying him.

The wind howled dismally without, and the rain beat furiously against the windows. I crept toward him and seated myself on a low stool beside his chair.

Presently he turned, without seeing me, and placed his foot absently in my lap. I affected not to notice it. But he started and looked down.

"You here yet — Carrothead? Ah, I forgot. Do you speak French?"

"*Oui, Monsieur.*"

"*Taisez-vous!*" he said sharply, with singular

purity of accent. I complied. The wind moaned
fearfully in the chimney, and the light burned
dimly. I shuddered in spite of myself. "Ah,
you tremble, girl!"

"It is a fearful night."

"Fearful! Call you this fearful, ha! ha! ha!
Look! you wretched little atom, look!" and he
dashed forward, and, leaping out of the window,
stood like a statue in the pelting storm, with
folded arms. He did not stay long, but in a few
minutes returned by way of the hall chimney. I
saw from the way that he wiped his feet on my
dress that he had again forgotten my presence.

"You are a governess. What can you teach?"
he asked, suddenly and fiercely thrusting his face
in mine.

"Manners!" I replied, calmly.

"Ha! teach *me*!"

"You mistake yourself," I said, adjusting my
mittens. "Your manners require not the artificial
restraint of society. You are radically polite; this
impetuosity and ferociousness is simply the sincerity which is the basis of a proper deportment.
Your instincts are moral; your better nature, I

see, is religious. As St. Paul justly remarks —
see chap. 6, 8, 9, and 10 — "

He seized a heavy candlestick, and threw it at
me. I dodged it submissively but firmly.

"Excuse me," he remarked, as his under jaw
slowly relaxed. "Excuse me, Miss Mix — but I
can't stand St. Paul! Enough — you are engaged."

CHAPTER IV.

I FOLLOWED the housekeeper as she led the way
timidly to my room. As we passed into a dark
hall in the wing, I noticed that it was closed by
an iron gate with a grating. Three of the doors
on the corridor were likewise grated. A strange
noise, as of shuffling feet and the howling of infuriated animals, rang through the hall. Bidding
the housekeeper good night, and taking the candle,
I entered my bedchamber.

I took off my dress, and, putting on a yellow
flannel nightgown, which I could not help feeling
did not agree with my complexion, I composed

myself to rest by reading *Blair's Rhetoric* and *Paley's Moral Philosophy.* I had just put out the light, when I heard voices in the corridor. I listened attentively. I recognized Mr. Rawjester's stern tones.

" Have you fed No. 1 ? " he asked.

"Yes, sir," said a gruff voice, apparently belonging to a domestic.

" How's No. 2 ? "

" She's a little off her feed, just now, but will pick up in a day or two ! "

" And No. 3 ? "

" Perfectly furious, sir. Her tantrums are ungovernable."

"Hush ! "

The voices died away, and I sank into a fitful slumber.

I dreamed that I was wandering through a tropical forest. Suddenly I saw the figure of a gorilla approaching me. As it neared me, I recognized the features of Mr. Rawjester. He held his hand to his side as if in pain. I saw that he had been wounded. He recognized me and called me by name, but at the same moment the vision changed to an Ashantee village, where, around the fire, a group of negroes were dancing and participating in some wild *Obi* festival. I awoke with the strain still ringing in my ears.

" Hokee-pokee wokee fum !"

Good Heavens ! could I be dreaming ? I heard the voice distinctly on the floor below, and smelt something burning. I arose, with an indistinct presentiment of evil, and hastily putting some cotton in my ears and tying a towel about my head, I wrapped myself in a shawl and rushed down stairs. The door of Mr. Rawjester's room was open. I entered.

Mr. Rawjester lay apparently in a deep slumber, from which even the clouds of smoke that came from the burning curtains of his bed could not rouse him. Around the room a large and power-ful negress, scantily attired, with her head adorned with feathers, was dancing wildly, accompanying herself with bone castanets. It looked like some terrible *fetich*.

I did not lose my calmness. After firmly empty-ing the pitcher, basin, and slop-jar on the burning bed, I proceeded cautiously to the garden, and, returning with the garden-engine, I directed a small stream at Mr. Rawjester.

At my entrance the gigantic negress fled. Mr. Rawjester yawned and woke. I explained to him, as he rose dripping from the bed, the reason of my presence. He did not seem to be excited, alarmed, or discomposed. He gazed at me curiously.

"So you risked your life to save mine, eh? you canary-colored teacher of infants."

I blushed modestly, and drew my shawl tightly over my yellow flannel nightgown.

"You love me, Mary Jane, — don't deny it! This trembling shows it!" He drew me closely toward him, and said, with his deep voice tenderly modulated : —

"How's her pooty tootens, — did she get her 'ittle tootens wet, — bess her?"

I understood his allusion to my feet. I glanced down and saw that in my hurry I had put on a pair of his old india-rubbers. My feet were not small or pretty, and the addition did not add to their beauty.

"Let me go, sir," I remarked quietly. "This is entirely improper; it sets a bad example for your child." And I firmly but gently extricated myself from his grasp. I approached the door. He seemed for a moment buried in deep thought.

"You say this was a negress?"

"Yes, sir."

"Humph, No. 1, I suppose?"

"Who is Number One, sir?"

"My *first*," he remarked, with a significant and sarcastic smile. Then, relapsing into his old manner, he threw his boots at my head, and bade me begone. I withdrew calmly.

CHAPTER V.

MY pupil was a bright little girl, who spoke French with a perfect accent. Her mother had been a French ballet-dancer, which probably accounted for it. Although she was only six years old, it was easy to perceive that she had been several times in love. She once said to me : —

"Miss Mix, did you ever have the *grande* passion? Did you ever feel a fluttering here?" and she placed her hand upon her small chest, and sighed quaintly, "a kind of distaste for *bonbons* and *caromels*, when the world seemed as tasteless and hollow as a broken cordial drop."

"Then you have felt it, Nina?" I said quietly.

"O dear, yes. There was Buttons, — that was our page, you know, — I loved him dearly, but papa sent him away. Then there was Dick, the groom, but he laughed at me, and I suffered misery!" and she struck a tragic French attitude. "There is to be company here to-morrow," she added, rattling on with childish *naïveté*, "and papa's sweetheart — Blanche Marabout — is to be here. You know they say she is to be my mamma."

What thrill was this shot through me? But I rose calmly, and, administering a slight correction to the child, left the apartment.

Blunderbore House, for the next week, was the scene of gayety and merriment. That portion of the mansion closed with a grating was walled up, and the midnight shrieks no longer troubled me.

But I felt more keenly the degradation of my situation. I was obliged to help Lady Blanche at her toilet and help her to look beautiful. For

what ?   To captivate him ?   O — no, no, — but
why this sudden thrill and faintness ?   Did he
really love her ?   I had seen him pinch and swear
at her.   But I reflected that he had thrown a candlestick at my head, and my foolish heart was re-
assured.

It was a night of festivity, when a sudden message obliged Mr. Rawjester to leave his guests for
a few hours.   " Make yourselves merry, idiots," he
added, under his breath, as he passed me.   The
door closed and he was gone.

An half-hour passed.   In the midst of the dancing a shriek was heard, and out of the swaying
crowd of fainting women and excited men a wild
figure strode into the room.   One glance showed
it to be a highwayman, heavily armed, holding a
pistol in each hand.

" Let no one pass out of this room ! " he said, in
a voice of thunder.   " The house is surrounded and
you cannot escape.   The first one who crosses yonder threshold will be shot like a dog.   Gentlemen,
I 'll trouble you to approach in single file, and hand
me your purses and watches."

Finding resistance useless, the order was ungraciously obeyed.

"Now, ladies, please to pass up your jewelry and trinkets."

This order was still more ungraciously complied with. As Blanche handed to the bandit captain her bracelet, she endeavored to conceal a diamond necklace, the gift of Mr. Rawjester, in her bosom. But, with a demoniac grin, the powerful brute tore it from its concealment, and, administering a hearty box on the ear of the young girl, flung her aside.

It was now my turn. With a beating heart I made my way to the robber chieftain, and sank at his feet. "O sir, I am nothing but a poor governess, pray let me go."

"O ho! A governess? Give me your last month's wages, then. Give me what you have stolen from your master!" and he laughed fiendishly.

I gazed at him quietly, and said, in a low voice: "I have stolen nothing from you, Mr. Rawjester!"

"Ah, discovered! Hush! listen, girl!" he hissed, in a fiercer whisper, "utter a syllable to frustrate my plans and you die; aid me, and — " But he was gone.

In a few moments the party, with the exception

of myself, were gagged and locked in the cellar. The next moment torches were applied to the rich hangings, and the house was in flames. I felt a strong hand seize me, and bear me out in the open air and place me upon the hillside, where I could overlook the burning mansion. It was Mr. Rawjester.

"Burn!" he said, as he shook his fist at the flames. Then sinking on his knees before me, he said hurriedly: —

"Mary Jane, I love you; the obstacles to our union are or will be soon removed. In yonder mansion were confined my three crazy wives. One of them, as you know, attempted to kill me! Ha! this is vengeance! But will you be mine?"

I fell, without a word, upon his neck.

GUY HEAVYSTONE;

OR,

"ENTIRE."

A MUSCULAR NOVEL.

BY THE AUTHOR OF "SWORD AND GUN."

------◆------

CHAPTER I.

"Nerei repandirostrum incurvicervicum pecus."

A DINGY, swashy, splashy afternoon in October;
a school-yard filled with a mob of riotous boys. A
lot of us standing outside.

Suddenly came a dull, crashing sound from the
school-room. At the ominous interruption I shuddered involuntarily, and called to Smithsye: —

"What's up, Smithums?"

"Guy's cleaning out the fourth form," he
replied.

At the same moment George de Coverly passed
me, holding his nose, from whence the bright Nor-

man blood streamed redly. To him the plebeian
Smithsye laughingly : —

"Cully ! how 's his nibs ? "

I pushed the door of the school-room open.
There are some spectacles which a man never
forgets. The burning of Troy probably seemed
a large-sized conflagration to the pious Æneas,
and made an impression on him which he carried
away with the feeble Anchises.

In the centre of the room, lightly brandishing
the piston-rod of a steam-engine, stood Guy Heavystone alone. I say alone, for the pile of small boys
on the floor in the corner could hardly be called
company.

I will try and sketch him for the reader. Guy
Heavystone was then only fifteen. His broad,
deep chest, his sinewy and quivering flank, his
straight pastern, showed him to be a thorough-
bred. Perhaps he was a trifle heavy in the fet-
lock, but he held his head haughtily erect. His
eyes were glittering but pitiless. There was a
sternness about the lower part of his face, — the
old Heavystone look, — a sternness, heightened,
perhaps, by the snaffle-bit which, in one of his

strange freaks, he wore in his mouth to curb his occasional ferocity. His dress was well adapted to his square-set and herculean frame. A striped knit undershirt, close-fitting striped tights, and a few spangles set off his figure; a neat Glengarry cap adorned his head. On it was displayed the Heavystone crest, a cock *regardant* on a dunghill *or*, and the motto, " Devil a better ! "

I thought of Horatius on the bridge, of Hector before the walls. I always make it a point to think of something classical at such times.

He saw me, and his sternness partly relaxed. Something like a smile struggled through his grim lineaments. It was like looking on the Jungfrau after having seen Mont Blanc, — a trifle, only a trifle less sublime and awful. Resting his hand lightly on the shoulder of the head-master, who shuddered and collapsed under his touch, he strode toward me.

His walk was peculiar. You could not call it a stride. It was like the " crest-tossing Bellerophon," — a kind of prancing gait. Guy Heavystone pranced toward me.

CHAPTER II.

"Lord Lovel he stood at the garden gate,
A-combing his milk-white steed."

IT was the winter of 186– when I next met Guy Heavystone. He had left the University and had entered the 76th "Heavies." "I have exchanged the gown for the sword, you see," he said, grasping my hand, and fracturing the bones of my little finger, as he shook it.

I gazed at him with unmixed admiration. He was squarer, sterner, and in every way smarter and more remarkable than ever. I began to feel toward this man as Phalaster felt towards Phyrgino, as somebody must have felt toward Archididasculus, as Boswell felt toward Johnson.

"Come into my den," he said, and lifting me gently by the seat of my pantaloons he carried me up stairs and deposited me, before I could apologize, on the sofa. I looked around the room. It was a bachelor's apartment, characteristically furnished in the taste of the proprietor. A few claymores and battle-axes were ranged against the wall, and a culverin, captured by Sir Ralph Heavystone, occupied the corner, the other end of the room being taken up by a light battery. Foils, boxing-gloves, saddles, and fishing-poles lay around carelessly. A small pile of billets-doux lay upon a silver salver. The man was not an anchorite, nor yet a Sir Galahad.

I never could tell what Guy thought of women. "Poor little beasts," he would often say when the conversation turned on any of his fresh conquests. Then, passing his hand over his marble brow, the old look of stern fixedness of purpose and unflinching severity would straighten the lines of his mouth, and he would mutter, half to himself, " S'death ! "

" Come with me to Heavystone Grange. The Exmoor Hounds throw off to-morrow. I 'll give you a mount," he said, as he amused himself by rolling up a silver candlestick between his fingers. " You shall have *Cleopatra*. But stay," he added, thoughtfully ; " now I remember, I ordered *Cleopatra* to be shot this morning "

" And why ? " I queried.

" She threw her rider yesterday and fell on him — "

" And killed him ? "

" No. That 's the reason why I have ordered her to be shot. I keep no animals that are not dangerous — I should add — *deadly !* " He hissed the last sentence between his teeth, and a gloomy frown descended over his calm brow.

I affected to turn over the tradesman's bills that lay on the table, for, like all of the Heavystone race, Guy seldom paid cash, and said : —

" You remind me of the time when Leonidas — "

" O, bother Leonidas and your classical allusions. Come ! "

We descended to dinner.

CHAPTER III.

" He carries weight, he rides a race,
'T is for a thousand pound."

" THERE is Flora Billingsgate, the greatest co- quette and hardest rider in the country," said my companion, Ralph Mortmain, as we stood upon Dingleby Common before the meet.

I looked up and beheld Guy Heavystone bending haughtily over the saddle, as he addressed a beautiful brunette. She was indeed a splendidly groomed and high-spirited woman. We were near enough to overhear the following conversation, which any high-toned reader will recognize as the common and natural expression of the higher classes.

"When Diana takes the field the chase is not wholly confined to objects *feræ naturæ*," said Guy, darting a significant glance at his companion. Flora did not shrink either from the glance or the meaning implied in the sarcasm.

"If I were looking for an Endymion, now — " she said archly, as she playfully cantered over a few hounds and leaped a five-barred gate.

Guy whispered a few words, inaudible to the rest of the party, and, curvetting slightly, cleverly cleared two of the huntsmen in a flying leap, galloped up the front steps of the mansion, and dashing at full speed through the hall leaped through the drawing-room window and rejoined me, languidly, on the lawn.

"Be careful of Flora Billingsgate," he said to me,

in low stern tones, while his pitiless eye shot a baleful fire. "*Gardez vous !*"

"*Gnothi seauton,*" I replied calmly, not wishing to appear to be behind him in perception or verbal felicity.

Guy started off in high spirits. He was well carried. He and the first whip, a ten-stone man, were head and head at the last fence, while the hounds were rolling over their fox a hundred yards farther in the open.

But an unexpected circumstance occurred. Coming back, his chestnut mare refused a ten-foot wall. She reared and fell backward. Again he led her up to it lightly; again she refused, falling heavily from the coping. Guy started to his feet. The old pitiless fire shone in his eyes; the old stern look settled around his mouth. Seizing the mare by the tail and mane he threw her over the wall. She landed twenty feet on the other side, erect and trembling. Lightly leaping the same obstacle himself, he remounted her. She did not refuse the wall the next time.

CHAPTER IV.

"He holds him by his glittering eye."

Guy was in the North of Ireland, cock-shooting. So Ralph Mortmain told me, and also that the match between Mary Brandagee and Guy had been broken off by Flora Billingsgate. "I don't like those Billingsgates," said Ralph, "they 're a bad stock. Her father, Smithfield de Billingsgate, had an unpleasant way of turning up the knave from the bottom of the pack. But *nous verrons;* let us go and see Guy."

The next morning we started for Fin-ma-Coul's Crossing. When I reached the shooting-box, where Guy was entertaining a select company of friends, Flora Billingsgate greeted me with a saucy smile.

Guy was even squarer and sterner than ever. His gusts of passion were more frequent, and it was with difficulty that he could keep an able-bodied servant in his family. His present retainers were more or less maimed from exposure to the fury of their master. There was a strange cynicism, a cutting sarcasm in his address, piercing through his polished manner. I thought of Timon, etc., etc.

One evening, we were sitting over our Chambertin, after a hard day's work, and Guy was listlessly turning over some letters, when suddenly he uttered a cry. Did you ever hear the trumpeting of a wounded elephant? It was like that.

I looked at him with consternation. He was glancing at a letter which he held at arm's length, and snorting, as it were, at it as he gazed. The lower part of his face was stern, but not as rigid as usual. He was slowly grinding between his teeth the fragments of the glass he had just been drinking from. Suddenly he seized one of his servants, and, forcing the wretch upon his knees, exclaimed, with the roar of a tiger : —

" Dog! why was this kept from me ? "

" Why, please, sir, Miss Flora said as how it was a reconciliation from Miss Brandagee, and it was to be kept from you where you would not be likely to see it, — and — and — "

" Speak, dog ! and you — "

"I put it among your bills, sir!"

With a groan, like distant thunder, Guy fell swooning to the floor.

He soon recovered, for the next moment a servant came rushing into the room with the information that a number of the ingenuous peasantry of the neighborhood were about to indulge that evening in the national pastime of burning a farm-house and shooting a landlord. Guy smiled a fearful smile, without, however, altering his stern and pitiless expression.

"Let them come," he said calmly; "I feel like entertaining company."

We barricaded the doors and windows, and then chose our arms from the armory. Guy's choice was a singular one : it was a landing net with a long handle, and a sharp cavalry sabre.

We were not destined to remain long in ignorance of its use. A howl was heard from without, and a party of fifty or sixty armed men precipitated themselves against the door.

Suddenly the window opened. With the rapidity of lightning, Guy Heavystone cast the net over the head of the ringleader, ejaculated "*Habet!*"

and with a back stroke of his cavalry sabre severed the member from its trunk, and, drawing the
net back again, cast the gory head upon the floor,
saying quietly : —

" One."

Again the net was cast, the steel flashed, the net
was withdrawn, and an ominous " Two ! " accompanied the head as it rolled on the floor.

" Do you remember what Pliny says of the
gladiator ? " said Guy, calmly wiping his sabre.
" How graphic is that passage commencing ' *Inter
nos, etc.*' " The sport continued until the heads of
twenty desperadoes had been gathered in. The
rest seemed inclined to disperse. Guy incautiously showed himself at the door; a ringing shot was
heard, and he staggered back, pierced through the
heart. Grasping the door-post in the last unconscious throes of his mighty frame, the whole side
of the house yielded to that earthquake tremor,
and we had barely time to escape before the whole
building fell in ruins. I thought of Samson, the
Giant Judge, etc., etc. ; but all was over.

Guy Heavystone had died as he had lived, —
hard.

MR. MIDSHIPMAN BREEZY.

A NAVAL OFFICER.

By CAPTAIN M—RRY—T, R. N.

CHAPTER I.

MY father was a north-country surgeon. He had retired, a widower, from her Majesty's navy many years before, and had a small practice in his native village. When I was seven years old he employed me to carry medicines to his patients. Being of a lively disposition, I sometimes amused myself, during my daily rounds, by mixing the contents of the different phials. Although I had no reason to doubt that the general result of this practice was beneficial, yet, as the death of a consumptive curate followed the addition of a strong mercurial lotion to his expectorant, my father concluded to withdraw me from the profession and send me to school.

Grubbins, the schoolmaster, was a tyrant, and it

was not long before my impetuous and self-willed
nature rebelled against his authority. I soon began to form plans of revenge. In this I was assisted by Tom Snaffle, — a schoolfellow. One day
Tom suggested : —

"Suppose we blow him up. I 've got two
pounds of powder !"

"No, that 's too noisy," I replied.

Tom was silent for a minute, and again spoke : —

"You remember how you flattened out the
curate, Pills ! Could n't you give Grubbins something — something to make him leathery sick —
eh ?"

A flash of inspiration crossed my mind. I went
to the shop of the village apothecary. He knew
me; I had often purchased vitriol, which I poured
into Grubbins's inkstand to corrode his pens and
burn up his coat-tail, on which he was in the
habit of wiping them. I boldly asked for an
ounce of chloroform. The young apothecary
winked and handed me the bottle.

It was Grubbins's custom to throw his handkerchief over his head, recline in his chair and take
a short nap during recess. Watching my oppor-

tunity, as he dozed, I managed to slip his handkerchief from his face and substitute my own,
moistened with chloroform. In a few minutes he
was insensible. Tom and I then quickly shaved
his head, beard, and eyebrows, blackened his face
with a mixture of vitriol and burnt cork, and
fled. There was a row and scandal the next day.
My father always excused me by asserting that
Grubbins had got drunk, — but somehow found it
convenient to procure me an appointment in her
Majesty's navy at an early day.

CHAPTER II.

AN official letter, with the Admiralty seal, informed me that I was expected to join H. M. ship
Belcher, Captain Boltrope, at Portsmouth, without
delay. In a few days I presented myself to a tall,
stern-visaged man, who was slowly pacing the lee-
ward side of the quarter-deck. As I touched my
hat he eyed me sternly : —

" So ho ! Another young suckling. The service
is going to the devil. Nothing but babes in the

cockpit and grannies in the board. Boatswain's mate, pass the word for Mr. Cheek!"

Mr. Cheek, the steward, appeared and touched his hat. "Introduce Mr. Breezy to the young gentlemen. Stop! Where's Mr. Swizzle?"

"At the masthead, sir."

"Where's Mr. Lankey?"

"At the masthead, sir."

"Mr. Briggs?"

"Masthead, too, sir."

"And the rest of the young gentlemen?" roared the enraged officer.

"All masthead, sir."

"Ah!" said Captain Boltrope, as he smiled grimly, "under the circumstances, Mr. Breezy, you had better go to the masthead too."

CHAPTER III.

AT the masthead I made the acquaintance of two youngsters of about my own age, one of whom informed me that he had been there three hundred and thirty-two days out of the year.

"In rough weather, when the old cock is out of sorts, you know, we never come down," added a young gentleman of nine years, with a dirk nearly as long as himself, who had been introduced to me as Mr. Briggs. "By the way, Pills," he continued, "how did you come to omit giving the captain a naval salute?"

"Why, I touched my hat," I said, innocently.

"Yes, but that is n't enough, you know. That will do very well at other times. He expects the naval salute when you first come on board — greeny!"

I began to feel alarmed, and begged him to explain.

"Why, you see, after touching your hat, you should have touched him lightly with your forefinger in his waistcoat, so, and asked, 'How 's his nibs?' — you see?"

"How 's his nibs?" I repeated.

"Exactly. He would have drawn back a little, and then you should have repeated the salute remarking, 'How 's his royal nibs?' asking cautiously after his wife and family, and requesting to be introduced to the gunner's daughter."

" The gunner's daughter ? "

" The same ; you know she takes care of us young gentlemen ; now don't forget, Pillsy ! "

When we were called down to the deck I thought it a good chance to profit by this instruction. I approached Captain Boltrope and repeated the salute without conscientiously omitting a single detail. He remained for a moment, livid and speechless. At length he gasped out : —

" Boatswain's mate ? "

" If you please, sir," I asked, tremulously, " I should like to be introduced to the gunner's daughter ! "

" O, very good, sir ! " screamed Captain Boltrope, rubbing his hands and absolutely capering about the deck with rage. " O d—n you ! Of course you shall ! O ho ! the gunner's daughter ! O, h—ll ! this is too much ! Boatswain's mate ! " Before I well knew where I was, I was seized, borne to an eight-pounder, tied upon it and flogged !

CHAPTER IV.

As we sat together in the cockpit, picking the weevils out of our biscuit, Briggs consoled me for my late mishap, adding that the "naval salute," as a custom, seemed just then to be honored more in the *breach* than the observance. I joined in the hilarity occasioned by the witticism, and in a few moments we were all friends. Presently Swizzle turned to me : —

"We have been just planning how to confiscate a keg of claret, which Nips, the purser, keeps under his bunk. The old nipcheese lies there drunk half the day, and there's no getting at it."

"Let's get beneath the state-room and bore through the deck, and so tap it," said Lankey.

The proposition was received with a shout of applause. A long half-inch auger and bit was procured from Chips, the carpenter's mate, and Swizzle, after a careful examination of the timbers beneath the ward-room, commenced operations. The auger at last disappeared, when suddenly there was a slight disturbance on the deck above. Swizzle withdrew the auger hurriedly ; from its point a few bright red drops trickled.

" Huzza ! send her up again !" cried Lankey.

The auger was again applied. This time a shriek was heard from the purser's cabin. Instantly the light was doused, and the party retreated hurriedly to the cockpit. A sound of snoring was heard as the sentry stuck his head into the door. " All right, sir," he replied in answer to the voice of the officer of the deck.

The next morning we heard that Nips was in the surgeon's hands, with a bad wound in the fleshy part of his leg, and that the auger had *not* struck claret.

CHAPTER V.

" Now, Pills, you 'll have a chance to smell powder," said Briggs as he entered the cockpit and buckled around his waist an enormous cutlass. " We have just sighted a French ship."

We went on deck. Captain Boltrope grinned

as we touched our hats. He hated the purser. "Come, young gentlemen, if you 're boring for French claret, yonder 's a good quality. Mind your con, sir," he added, turning to the quartermaster, who was grinning.

The ship was already cleared for action. The men, in their eagerness, had started the coffee from the tubs and filled them with shot. Presently the Frenchman yawed, and a shot from a long thirty-two came skipping over the water. It killed the quartermaster and took off both of Lankey's legs. "Tell the purser our account is squared," said the dying boy, with a feeble smile.

The fight raged fiercely for two hours. I remember killing the French Admiral, as we boarded, but on looking around for Briggs, after the smoke had cleared away, I was intensely amused at witnessing the following novel sight:—

Briggs had pinned the French captain against the mast with his cutlass, and was now engaged, with all the hilarity of youth, in pulling the captain's coat-tails between his legs, in imitation of a dancing-jack. As the Frenchman lifted his legs and arms, at each jerk of Briggs's, I could not help participating in the general mirth.

"You young devil, what are you doing?" said a stifled voice behind me. I looked up and beheld Captain Boltrope, endeavoring to calm his stern features, but the twitching around his mouth betrayed his intense enjoyment of the scene. "Go to the masthead — up with you, sir!" he repeated sternly to Briggs.

"Very good, sir," said the boy, coolly preparing to mount the shrouds. "Good by, Johnny Crapaud. Humph!" he added, in a tone intended for my ear, "a pretty way to treat a hero. The service is going to the devil!"

I thought so too.

CHAPTER VI.

WE were ordered to the West Indies. Although Captain Boltrope's manner toward me was still severe, and even harsh, I understood that my name had been favorably mentioned in the despatches.

Reader, were you ever at Jamaica? If so, you

remember the negresses, the oranges, Port Royal
Tom — the yellow fever.   After being two weeks
at the station, I was taken sick of the fever.   In a
month I was delirious.   During my paroxysms,
I had a wild distempered dream of a stern face
bending anxiously over my pillow, a rough hand
smoothing my hair, and a kind voice saying : —

"Bess his 'ittle heart! Did he have the naughty fever?" This face seemed again changed to
the well-known stern features of Captain Boltrope.

When I was convalescent, a packet edged in
black was put in my hand. It contained the
news of my father's death, and a sealed letter
which he had requested to be given to me on
his decease. I opened it tremblingly. It read
thus : —

"*My dear Boy* : — I regret to inform you that in all prob-
ability you are not my son. Your mother, I am grieved to
say, was a highly improper person. Who your father may
be, I really cannot say, but perhaps the Honorable Henry
Boltrope, Captain R. N., may be able to inform you. Circumstances over which I have no control have deferred
this important disclosure.

"YOUR STRICKEN PARENT."

And so Captain Boltrope was my father.   Heavens! Was it a dream? I recalled his stern manner, his observant eye, his ill-concealed uneasiness when in my presence. I longed to embrace him. Staggering to my feet, I rushed in my scanty apparel to the deck, where Captain Boltrope was just then engaged in receiving the Governor's wife and daughter. The ladies shrieked; the youngest, a beautiful girl, blushed deeply. Heeding them not, I sank at his feet, and, embracing them, cried: —

"My father!"

"Chuck him overboard!" roared Captain Boltrope.

"Stay," pleaded the soft voice of Clara Maitland, the Governor's daughter.

"Shave his head! he's a wretched lunatic!" continued Captain Boltrope, while his voice trembled with excitement.

"No, let me nurse and take care of him," said the lovely girl, blushing as she spoke. "Mamma, can't we take him home?"

The daughter's pleading was not without effect. In the mean time I had fainted. When I recovered my senses I found myself in Governor Maitland's mansion.

CHAPTER VII.

THE reader will guess what followed. I fell deeply in love with Clara Maitland, to whom I confided the secret of my birth. The generous girl asserted that she had detected the superiority of my manner at once. We plighted our troth, and resolved to wait upon events.

Briggs called to see me a few days afterward. He said that the purser had insulted the whole cockpit, and all the midshipmen had called him out. But he added thoughtfully: " I don't see how we can arrange the duel. You see there are six of us to fight him."

" Very easily," I replied. " Let your fellows all stand in a row, and take his fire; that, you see, gives him six chances to one, and he must be a bad shot if he can't hit one of you ; while, on the other hand, you see, he gets a volley from you six, and one of you 'll be certain to fetch him."

" Exactly " ; and away Briggs went, but soon returned to say that the purser had declined, — " like a d—d coward," he added.

But the news of the sudden and serious illness of Captain Boltrope put off the duel. I hastened to his bedside, but too late, — an hour previous he had given up the ghost.

I resolved to return to England. I made known the secret of my birth, and exhibited my adopted father's letter to Lady Maitland, who at once suggested my marriage with her daughter, before I returned to claim the property. We were married, and took our departure next day.

I made no delay in posting at once, in company with my wife and my friend Briggs, to my native village. Judge of my horror and surprise when my late adopted father came out of his shop to welcome me.

"Then you are not dead!" I gasped.

"No, my dear boy."

"And this letter?"

My father — as I must still call him — glanced on the paper, and pronounced it a forgery. Briggs roared with laughter. I turned to him and demanded an explanation.

"Why, don't you see, Greeny, it's all a joke, — a midshipman's joke!"

"But — " I asked.

"Don't be a fool. You 've got a good wife, — be satisfied."

I turned to Clara, and was satisfied. Although Mrs. Maitland never forgave me, the jolly old Governor laughed heartily over the joke, and so well used his influence that I soon became, dear reader, Admiral Breezy, K. C. B.

JOHN JENKINS;

OR,

THE SMOKER REFORMED.

By T. S. A—TH—R.

———◆———

CHAPTER I.

"ONE cigar a day !" said Judge Boompointer.

"One cigar a day !" repeated John Jenkins, as with trepidation he dropped his half-consumed cigar under his work-bench.

"One cigar a day is three cents a day," remarked Judge Boompointer, gravely ; "and do you know, sir, what one cigar a day, or three cents a day, amounts to in the course of four years ? "

John Jenkins, in his boyhood, had attended the village school, and possessed considerable arithmetical ability. Taking up a shingle which lay upon his work-bench, and producing a piece of chalk, with a feeling of conscious pride he made an exhaustive calculation.

"Exactly forty-three dollars and eighty cents,"

he replied, wiping the perspiration from his heated brow, while his face flushed with honest enthusiasm.

" Well, sir, if you saved three cents a day, instead of wasting it, you would now be the possessor of a new suit of clothes, an illustrated Family Bible, a pew in the church, a complete set of Patent Office Reports, a hymn-book, and a paid subscription to *Arthur's Home Magazine,* which could be purchased for exactly forty-three dollars and eighty cents ; and," added the Judge, with increasing sternness, " if you calculate leap-year, which you seem to have strangely omitted, you have three cents more, sir ; *three cents more !* What would that buy you, sir ? "

" A cigar," suggested John Jenkins ; but, coloring again deeply, he hid his face.

" No, sir," said the Judge, with a sweet smile of benevolence stealing over his stern features ; " properly invested, it would buy you that which passeth all price. Dropped into the missionary-box, who can tell what heathen, now idly and joyously wantoning in nakedness and sin, might be brought to a sense of his miserable condition, and made, through that three cents, to feel the torments of the wicked ? "

With these words the Judge retired, leaving John Jenkins buried in profound thought. " Three cents a day," he muttered.   " In forty years I might be worth four hundred and thirty-eight dollars and ten cents, — and then I might marry Mary. Ah, Mary ! " The young carpenter sighed, and, drawing a twenty-five cent daguerreotype from his vest-pocket, gazed long and fervidly upon the features of a young girl in book muslin and a coral neck-lace. Then, with a resolute expression, he carefully locked the door of his workshop and departed.

Alas ' his good resolutions were too late. We trifle with the tide of fortune which too often nips us in the bud and casts the dark shadow of misfortune over the bright lexicon of youth ! That night the half-consumed fragment of John Jenkins's cigar set fire to his workshop and burned it up, together with all his tools and materials. There was no insurance.

CHAPTER II.

THE DOWNWARD PATH.

"THEN you still persist in marrying John Jenkins?" queried Judge Boompointer, as he playfully, with paternal familiarity, lifted the golden curls of the village belle, Mary Jones.

"I do," replied the fair young girl, in a low voice, that resembled rock candy in its saccharine firmness, — "I do. He has promised to reform. Since he lost all his property by fire — ".

"The result of his pernicious habit, though he illogically persists in charging it to me," interrupted the Judge.

"Since then," continued the young girl, "he has endeavored to break himself of the habit. He tells me that he has substituted the stalks of the Indian ratan, the outer part of a leguminous plant called the smoking-bean, and the fragmentary and unconsumed remainder of cigars which occur at rare and uncertain intervals along the road, which, as he informs me, though deficient in quality and strength, are comparatively inexpensive." And, blushing at her own eloquence, the young girl hid her curls on the Judge's arm.

"Poor thing!" muttered Judge Boompointer. "Dare I tell her all? Yet I must."

"I shall cling to him," continued the young girl, rising with her theme, "as the young vine clings to some hoary ruin. Nay, nay, chide me not, Judge Boompointer. I will marry John Jenkins!"

The Judge was evidently affected. Seating himself at the table, he wrote a few lines hurriedly upon a piece of paper, which he folded and placed in the fingers of the destined bride of John Jenkins.

"Mary Jones," said the Judge, with impressive earnestness, "take this trifle as a wedding gift from one who respects your fidelity and truthfulness. At the altar let it be a reminder of me." And covering his face hastily with a handkerchief, the stern and iron-willed man left the room. As the door closed, Mary unfolded the paper. It was an order on the corner grocery for three yards of flannel, a paper of needles, four pounds of soap, one pound of starch, and two boxes of matches!

"Noble and thoughtful man!" was all Mary Jones could exclaim, as she hid her face in her hands and burst into a flood of tears.

*   *   *   *   *

The bells of Cloverdale are ringing merrily. It is a wedding. "How beautiful they look!" is the exclamation that passes from lip to lip, as Mary Jones, leaning timidly on the arm of John Jenkins, enters the church. But the bride is agitated, and the bridegroom betrays a feverish nervousness. As they stand in the vestibule, John Jenkins fumbles earnestly in his vest-pocket. Can it be the ring he is anxious about? No. He draws a small brown substance from his pocket, and biting off a piece, hastily replaces the fragment and gazes furtively around. Surely no one saw him? Alas! the eyes of two of that wedding party saw the fatal act. Judge Boompointer shook his head sternly. Mary Jones sighed and breathed a silent prayer. Her husband chewed!

CHAPTER III. AND LAST.

"WHAT! more bread?" said John Jenkins, gruffly. "You 're always asking for money for bread.
D—nation! Do you want to ruin me by your extravagance?" and as he uttered these words he
drew from his pocket a bottle of whiskey, a pipe,
and a paper of tobacco. Emptying the first at a
draught, he threw the empty bottle at the head of
his eldest boy, a youth of twelve summers. The
missile struck the child full in the temple, and
stretched him a lifeless corpse. Mrs. Jenkins,
whom the reader will hardly recognize as the once
gay and beautiful Mary Jones, raised the dead
body of her son in her arms, and carefully placing
the unfortunate youth beside the pump in the
back yard, returned with saddened step to the
house. At another time, and in brighter days, she
might have wept at the occurrence. She was past
tears now.

"Father, your conduct is reprehensible!" said

little Harrison Jenkins, the youngest boy. "Where do you expect to go when you die?"

"Ah!" said John Jenkins, fiercely; "this comes of giving children a liberal education; this is the result of Sabbath schools. Down, viper!"

A tumbler thrown from the same parental fist laid out the youthful Harrison cold. The four other children had, in the mean time, gathered around the table with anxious expectancy. With a chuckle, the now changed and brutal John Jenkins produced four pipes, and, filling them with tobacco, handed one to each of his offspring and bade them smoke. "It's better than bread!" laughed the wretch hoarsely.

Mary Jenkins, though of a patient nature, felt it her duty now to speak. "I have borne much, John Jenkins," she said. "But I prefer that the children should not smoke. It is an unclean habit, and soils their clothes. I ask this as a special favor!"

John Jenkins hesitated, — the pangs of remorse began to seize him.

"Promise me this, John!" urged Mary upon her knees.

6—v. 5

"I promise!" reluctantly answered John.

"And you will put the money in a savings-bank?"

"I will," repeated her husband; "and *I*'ll give up smoking, too."

"'T is well, John Jenkins!" said Judge Boompointer, appearing suddenly from behind the door, where he had been concealed during this interview. "Nobly said! my man. Cheer up! I will see that the children are decently buried." The husband and wife fell into each other's arms. And Judge Boompointer, gazing upon the affecting spectacle, burst into tears.

From that day John Jenkins was an altered man.

NO TITLE.

By W—LK—E C—LL—NS.

PROLOGUE.

THE following advertisement appeared in the
" Times " of the 17th of June, 1845 : —

WANTED. — A few young men for a light genteel employment.   Address
J. W., P. O.

In the same paper, of same date, in another
column : —

TO LET. — That commodious and elegant family mansion,
No. 27 Limehouse Road, Pultneyville, will be rented low to
a respectable tenant if applied for immediately, the family being
about to remove to the continent.

Under the local intelligence, in another column : —

MISSING. — An unknown elderly gentleman a week ago left
his lodgings in the Kent Road, since which nothing has been
heard of him.   He left no trace of his identity except a port-
manteau containing a couple of shirts marked " 209, WARD."

To find the connection between the mysterious
disappearance of the elderly gentleman and the
anonymous communication, the relevancy of both

these incidents to the letting of a commodious
family mansion, and the dead secret involved in
the three occurrences, is the task of the writer
of this history.

A slim young man with spectacles, a large hat,
drab gaiters, and a note-book, sat late that night
with a copy of the "Times" before him, and a
pencil which he rattled nervously between his
teeth in the coffee-room of the "Blue Dragon."

CHAPTER I.

MARY JONES'S NARRATIVE.

I AM upper housemaid to the family that live
at No. 27 Limehouse Road, Pultneyville. I have
been requested by Mr. Wilkey Collings, which I
takes the liberty of here stating is a gentleman
born and bred, and has some consideration for the
feelings of servants, and is not above rewarding
them for their trouble, which is more than you
can say for some who ask questions and gets short
answers enough, gracious knows, to tell what I
know about them. I have been requested to tell

my story in my own langwidge, though, being no schollard, mind cannot conceive. I think my master is a brute. Do not know that he has ever attempted to poison my missus, — which is too good for him, and how she ever came to marry him, heart only can tell, — but believe him to be capable of any such hatrosity. Have heard him swear dreadful because of not having his shaving-water at nine o'clock precisely. Do not know whether he ever forged a will or tried to get my missus' property, although, not having confidence in the man, should not be surprised if he had done so. Believe that there was always something mysterious in his conduct. Remember distinctly how the family left home to go abroad. Was putting up my back hair, last Saturday morning, when I heard a ring. Says cook, "That's missus' bell, and mind you hurry or the master 'ill know why." Says I, "Humbly thanking you, mem, but taking advice of them as is competent to give it, I'll take my time." Found missus dressing herself and master growling as usual. Says missus, quite calm and easy like, "Mary, we begin to pack to-day." "What for, mem?" says I, taken aback.

"What's that hussy asking?" says master from the bedclothes quite savage like. "For the Continent—Italy," says missus—"Can you go Mary?" Her voice was quite gentle and saintlike, but I knew the struggle it cost, and says I, "With *you* mem, to India's torrid clime, if required, but with African Gorillas," says I, looking toward the bed, "never." "Leave the room," says master, starting up and catching of his bootjack. "Why Charles!" says missus, "how you talk!" affecting surprise. "Do go Mary," says she, slipping a half-crown into my hand. I left the room scorning to take notice of the odious wretch's conduct.

Cannot say whether my master and missus were ever legally married. What with the dreadful state of morals nowadays and them stories in the circulating libraries, innocent girls don't know into what society they might be obliged to take situations. Never saw missus' marriage certificate, though I have quite accidental-like looked in her desk when open, and would have seen it. Do not know of any lovers missus might have had. Believe she had a liking for John Thomas, footman, for she was always spiteful-like — poor lady —

when we were together — though there was nothing between us, as Cook well knows, and dare not
deny, and missus need n't have been jealous.
Have never seen arsenic or Prussian acid in any
of the private drawers — but have seen paregoric
and camphor. One of my master's friends was a
Count Moscow, a Russian papist — which I de-
tested.

CHAPTER II.

THE SLIM YOUNG MAN'S STORY.

I AM by profession a reporter, and writer for the
press. I live at Pultneyville. I have always had
a passion for the marvellous, and have been distinguished for my facility in tracing out mysteries,
and solving enigmatical occurrences. On the night
of the 17th June, 1845, I left my office and walked
homeward. The night was bright and starlight. I
was revolving in my mind the words of a singular
item I had just read in the "Times." I had reached
the darkest portion of the road, and found myself
mechanically repeating: " An elderly gentleman a

week ago left his lodgings on the Kent Road," when suddenly I heard a step behind me.

I turned quickly, with an expression of horror in my face, and by the light of the newly risen moon beheld an elderly gentleman, with green cotton umbrella, approaching me. His hair, which was snow white, was parted over a broad, open forehead. The expression of his face, which was slightly flushed, was that of amiability verging almost upon imbecility. There was a strange, inquiring look about the widely opened mild blue eye, — a look that might have been intensified to insanity, or modified to idiocy. As he passed me, he paused and partly turned his face, with a gesture of inquiry. I see him still, his white locks blowing in the evening breeze, his hat a little on the back of his head, and his figure painted in relief against the dark blue sky.

Suddenly he turned his mild eye full upon me. A weak smile played about his thin lips. In a voice which had something of the tremulousness of age and the self-satisfied chuckle of imbecility in it, he asked, pointing to the rising moon, " Why ? — Hush !"

He had dodged behind me, and appeared to be
ᴗwn the road. I could feel his
with terror as he laid his thin
ᴗulders and faced me in the
ᴗosed danger.

ᴗot hear them coming ? "
was no sound but the sough-
trees in the evening wind. I
ᴗre him, with such success that
ᴗhe old weak smile appeared on
ᴗ.

ᴗt the look of interrogation was
ᴗeless blankness.

ᴗated with assuring accents.

ᴗ, a gleam of intelligence flicker-
" is yonder moon, as she sails in
the blue empyrean, casting a flood of light o'er
hill and dale, like — Why," he repeated, with a
feeble smile, " is yonder moon, as she sails in the
blue empyrean — " He hesitated, — stammered,
— and gazed at me hopelessly, with the tears dripping from his moist and widely opened eyes.

I took his hand kindly in my own. " Casting a

shadow o'er hill and dale," I repeated quietly, leading him up the subject, "like — Come, now."

"Ah!" he said, pressing my hand tremulously, "you know it?"

"I do. Why is it like — the — eh — the commodious mansion on the Limehouse Road?"

A blank stare only followed. He shook his head sadly. "Like the young men wanted for a light, genteel employment?"

He wagged his feeble old head cunningly.

"Or, Mr. Ward," I said, with bold confidence, "like the mysterious disappearance from the Kent Road?"

The moment was full of suspense. He did not seem to hear me. Suddenly he turned.

"Ha!"

I darted forward. But he had vanished in the darkness.

CHAPTER III.

NO. 27 LIMEHOUSE ROAD.

It was a hot midsummer evening. Limehouse Road was deserted save by dust and a few rattling butchers' carts, and the bell of the muffin and crumpet man. A commodious mansion, which stood on the right of the road as you enter Pultneyville, surrounded by stately poplars and a high fence surmounted by a *chevaux de frise* of broken glass, looked to the passing and footsore pedestrian like the genius of seclusion and solitude. A bill announcing in the usual terms that the house was to let, hung from the bell at the servants' entrance.

As the shades of evening closed, and the long shadows of the poplars stretched across the road, a man carrying a small kettle stopped and gazed, first at the bill and then at the house. When he had reached the corner of the fence, he again stopped and looked cautiously up and down the road. Apparently satisfied with the result of his scrutiny, he deliberately sat himself down in the

dark shadow of the fence, and at once busied himself in some employment, so well concealed as to
be invisible to the gaze of passers-by.   At the end
of an hour he retired cautiously.

But not altogether unseen.   A slim young man,
with spectacles and note-book, stepped from behind a tree as the retreating figure of the intruder
was lost in the twilight, and transferred from the
fence to his note-book the freshly stencilled inscription, " S — T — 1860 — X."

CHAPTER IV.

COUNT MOSCOW'S NARRATIVE.

I AM a foreigner.   Observe !   To be a foreigner
in England is to be mysterious, suspicious, intrigu-
ing.   M. Collins has requested the history of my
complicity with certain occurrences.   It is nothing, bah ! absolutely nothing.

I write with ease and fluency.   Why should I
not write ?   Tra la la !   I am what you English
call corpulent.   Ha, ha !   I am a pupil of Macchiavelli.   I find it much better to disbelieve every-

thing, and to approach my subject and wishes circuitously, than in a direct manner. You have observed that playful animal, the cat. Call it, and it does not come to you directly, but rubs itself against all the furniture in the room, and reaches you finally — and scratches. Ah, ha, scratches! I am of the feline species. People call me a villain — bah!

I know the family, living No. 27 Limehouse Road. I respect the gentleman, — a fine, burly specimen of your Englishman, — and madame, charming, ravishing, delightful. When it became known to me that they designed to let their delightful residence, and visit foreign shores, I at once called upon them. I kissed the hand of madame. I embraced the great Englishman. Madame blushed slightly. The great Englishman shook my hand like a mastiff.

I began in that dexterous, insinuating manner, of which I am truly proud. I thought madame was ill. Ah, no. A change, then, was all that was required. I sat down at the piano and sang. In a few minutes madame retired. I was alone with my friend.

Seizing his hand, I began with every demonstration of courteous sympathy. I do not repeat my words, for my intention was conveyed more in accent, emphasis, and manner, than speech. I hinted to him that he had another wife living. I suggested that this was balanced — ha ! — by his wife's lover. That, possibly, he wished to fly ; hence the letting of his delightful mansion. That he regularly and systematically beat his wife in the English manner, and that she repeatedly deceived me. I talked of hope, of consolation, of remedy. I carelessly produced a bottle of strychnine and a small vial of stramonium from my pocket, and enlarged on the efficiency of drugs. His face, which had gradually become convulsed, suddenly became fixed with a frightful expression. He started to his feet, and roared : " You d—d Frenchman ! "

I instantly changed my tactics, and endeavored to embrace him. He kicked me twice, violently. I begged permission to kiss madame's hand. He replied by throwing me down stairs.

I am in bed with my head bound up, and beefsteaks upon my eyes, but still confident and buoyant. I have not lost faith in Macchiavelli. Tra la la ! as they sing in the opera. I kiss everybody's hands.

CHAPTER V.

DR. DIGGS'S STATEMENT.

MY name is David Diggs. I am a surgeon, living at No. 9 Tottenham Court. On the 15th of June, 1854, I was called to see an elderly gentleman lodging on the Kent Road. Found him highly excited, with strong febrile symptoms, pulse 120, increasing. Repeated incoherently what I judged to be the popular form of a conundrum. On closer examination found acute hydrocephalus and both lobes of the brain rapidly filling with water. In consultation with an eminent phrenologist, it was further discovered that all the organs were more or less obliterated, except that of Comparison. Hence the patient was enabled to only distinguish the most common points of resemblance between objects, without drawing upon other faculties, such as Ideality or Language,

for assistance.   Later in the day found him sinking, — being evidently unable to carry the most
ordinary conundrum to a successful issue.   Exhibited Tinct. Val., Ext. Opii, and Camphor, and pre-
scribed quiet and emollients.   On the 17th the
patient was missing.

CHAPTER LAST.

STATEMENT OF THE PUBLISHER.

ON the 18th of June, Mr. Wilkie Collins left a
roll of manuscript with us for publication, without
title or direction, since which time he has not
been heard from.   In spite of the care of the
proof-readers, and valuable literary assistance, it
is feared that the continuity of the story has been
destroyed by some accidental misplacing of chapters during its progress.   How and what chapters
are so misplaced, the publisher leaves to an indul-
gent public to discover.

N N.

BEING A NOVEL IN THE FRENCH PARAGRAPHIC STYLE.

———◆———

— MADEMOISELLE, I swear to you that I love you.

— You who read these pages. You who turn your burning eyes upon these words — words that I trace — Ah, Heaven! the thought maddens me.

— I will be calm. I will imitate the reserve of the festive Englishman, who wears a spotted hand-kerchief which he calls a *Belchio*, who eats *biftek*, and caresses a bulldog. I will subdue myself like him.

— Ha! Poto-beer! All right — Goddam!

— Or, I will conduct myself as the free-born American — the gay Brother Jonathan! I will whittle me a stick. I will whistle to myself

" Yankee Doodle," and forget my passion in excessive expectoration.

— Hoho ! — wake snakes and walk chalks.

THE world is divided into two great divisions, —
Paris and the provinces.   There is but one Paris.
There are several provinces, among which may be
numbered England, America, Russia, and Italy.

N N. was a Parisian.

But N N. did not live in Paris.   Drop a Parisian in the provinces, and you drop a part of Paris
with him.   Drop him in Senegambia, and in three
days he will give you an *omelette soufflée*, or a *pâté
de foie gras*, served by the neatest of Senegambian
filles, whom he will call Mademoiselle.   In three
weeks he will give you an opera.

N N. was not dropped in Senegambia, but in
San Francisco, — quite as awkward.

They find gold in San Francisco, but they don't
understand gilding.

N N. existed three years in this place.   He became bald on the top of his head, as all Parisians
do.   Look down from your box at the Opera
Comique, Mademoiselle, and count the bald crowns

of the fast young men in the pit. Ah — you
tremble ! They show where the arrows of love
have struck and glanced off.

N N. was also near-sighted, as all Parisians
finally become. This is a gallant provision of Nature to spare them the mortification of observing
that their lady friends grow old. After a certain
age every woman is handsome to a Parisian.

One day, N N. was walking down Washington
street. Suddenly he stopped.

He was standing before the door of a mantuamaker. Beside the counter, at the farther extrem-
ity of the shop, stood a young and elegantly formed
woman. Her face was turned from N N. He
entered. With a plausible excuse, and seeming in-
difference, he gracefully opened conversation with
the mantuamaker as only a Parisian can. But he
had to deal with a Parisian. His attempts to view
the features of the fair stranger by the counter were
deftly combated by the shop-woman. He was
obliged to retire.

N N. went home and lost his appetite. He was
haunted by the elegant basque and graceful shoulders of the fair unknown, during the whole night.

The next day he sauntered by the mantuamaker. Ah! Heavens! A thrill ran through his
frame, and his fingers tingled with a delicious electricity. The fair *inconnue* was there! He raised
his hat gracefully. He was not certain, but he
thought that a slight motion of her faultless bonnet betrayed recognition. He would have wildly
darted into the shop, but just then the figure of
the mantuamaker appeared in the doorway.

— Did Monsieur wish anything?

Misfortune! Desperation. N N. purchased a
bottle of Prussic acid, a sack of charcoal, and a
quire of pink note-paper, and returned home. He
wrote a letter of farewell to the closely fitting
basque, and opened the bottle of Prussic acid.

Some one knocked at his door. It was a Chinaman, with his weekly linen.

These Chinese are docile, but not intelligent.
They are ingenious, but not creative. They are
cunning in expedients, but deficient in tact. In
love they are simply barbarous. They purchase
their wives openly, and not constructively by at-
torney. By offering small sums for their sweet-
hearts, they degrade the value of the sex.

Nevertheless, N N. felt he was saved. He explained all to the faithful Mongolian, and exhibited the letter he had written. He implored him to deliver it.

The Mongolian assented. The race are not cleanly or sweet-savored, but N N. fell upon his neck. He embraced him with one hand, and closed his nostrils with the other. Through him, he felt he clasped the close-fitting basque.

The next day was one of agony and suspense. Evening came, but no Mercy. N N. lit the charcoal. But, to compose his nerves, he closed his door and first walked mildly up and down Montgomery Steeet. When he returned, he found the faithful Mongolian on the steps.

— All lity !

These Chinese are not accurate in their pronunciation. They avoid the *r*, like the English nobleman.

N N. gasped for breath. He leaned heavily against the Chinaman.

— Then you have seen her, Ching Long ?

— Yes. All lity. She cum. Top side of house.

The docile barbarian pointed up the stairs, and chuckled.

— She here — impossible! Ah, Heaven! do I dream?

— Yes. All lity, — top side of house. Good by, John.

This is the familiar parting epithet of the Mongolian. It is equivalent to our *au revoir.*

N N. gazed with a stupefied air on the departing servant.

He placed his hand on his throbbing heart. She here, — alone beneath this roof. O Heavens, — what happiness!

But how? Torn from her home. Ruthlessly dragged, perhaps, from her evening devotions, by the hands of a relentless barbarian. Could she forgive him?

He dashed frantically up the stairs. He opened the door. She was standing beside his couch with averted face.

A strange giddiness overtook him. He sank upon his knees at the threshold.

— Pardon, pardon. My angel, can you forgive me?

A terrible nausea now seemed added to the fearful giddiness. His utterance grew thick and sluggish.

— Speak, speak, enchantress. Forgiveness is all I ask. My Love, my Life!

She did not answer. He staggered to his feet. As he rose, his eyes fell on the pan of burning charcoal. A terrible suspicion flashed across his mind. This giddiness, — this nausea. The ignorance of the barbarian. This silence. O merciful heavens! she was dying!

He crawled toward her. He touched her. She fell forward with a lifeless sound upon the floor. He uttered a piercing shriek, and threw himself beside her.

*   *   *   *   *

A file of gendarmes, accompanied by the *Chef* Burke, found him the next morning lying lifeless upon the floor. They laughed brutally, — these cruel minions of the law, — and disengaged his arm from the waist of the wooden dummy which they had come to reclaim for the mantuamaker.

Emptying a few bucketfuls of water over his form, they finally succeeded in robbing him, not only of his mistress, but of that Death he had coveted without her.

Ah! we live in a strange world, Messieurs.

FANTINE.

AFTER THE FRENCH OF VICTOR HUGO.

PROLOGUE.

As long as there shall exist three paradoxes, a moral Frenchman, a religious Atheist, and a believing sceptic; so long, in fact, as booksellers shall wait — say twenty-five years — for a new gospel; so long as paper shall remain cheap and ink three *sous* a bottle, I have no hesitation in saying that such books as these are not utterly profitless.

VICTOR HUGO.

I.

To be good is to be queer. What is a good man? Bishop Myriel.

My friend, you will possibly object to this. You will say you know what a good man is. Perhaps you will say your clergyman is a good man, for instance.

Bah! you are mistaken; you are an Englishman, and an Englishman is a beast.

Englishmen think they are moral when they are

only serious. These Englishmen also wear ill-shaped hats, and dress horribly!

Bah! they are *canaille*.

Still, Bishop Myriel was a good man, — quite as good as you. Better than you, in fact.

One day M. Myriel was in Paris. This angel used to walk about the streets like any other man. He was not proud, though fine-looking. Well, three *gamins de Paris* called him bad names. Says one : —

" Ah, *mon Dieu !* there goes a priest ; look out for your eggs and chickens ! "

What did this good man do ? He called to them kindly.

" My children," said he, " this is clearly not your fault. I recognize in this insult and irreverence only the fault of your immediate progenitors. Let us pray for your immediate progenitors."

They knelt down and prayed for their immediate progenitors.

The effect was touching.

The Bishop looked calmly around.

" On reflection," said he, gravely, " I was mistaken ; this is clearly the fault of Society. Let us pray for Society."

They knelt down and prayed for Society.

The effect was sublimer yet. What do you think of that? You, I mean.

Everybody remembers the story of the Bishop and Mother Nez Retroussé. Old Mother Nez Retroussé sold asparagus. She was poor; there's a great deal of meaning in that word, my friend. Some people say "poor but honest." I say, Bah!

Bishop Myriel bought six bunches of asparagus. This good man had one charming failing; he was fond of asparagus. He gave her a *franc* and received three *sous* change.

The *sous* were bad, — counterfeit. What did this good Bishop do? He said: "I should not have taken change from a poor woman."

Then afterwards, to his housekeeper: "Never take change from a poor woman."

Then he added to himself: "For the *sous* will probably be bad."

II.

WHEN a man commits a crime, society claps him in prison. A prison is one of the worst hotels imaginable. The people there are low and vulgar.

The butter is bad, the coffee is green. Ah, it is horrible!

In prison, as in a bad hotel, a man soon loses, not only his morals, but what is much worse to a Frenchman, his sense of refinement and delicacy.

Jean Valjean came from prison with confused notions of society. He forgot the modern peculiarities of hospitality. So he walked off with the Bishop's candlesticks.

Let us consider: candlesticks were stolen; that was evident. Society put Jean Valjean in prison; that was evident, too. In prison, Society took away his refinement; that is evident, likewise.

Who is Society?

You and I are Society.

My friend, you and I stole those candlesticks!

III.

THE Bishop thought so, too. He meditated profoundly for six days. On the morning of the seventh he went to the Prefecture of Police.

He said: "Monsieur, have me arrested. I have stolen candlesticks."

The official was governed by the law of Society, and refused.

What did this Bishop do ?

He had a charming ball and chain made, affixed to his leg, and wore it the rest of his life.

This is a fact !

IV.

LOVE is a mystery.

A little friend of mine down in the country, at Auvergne, said to me one day: "Victor, Love is the world, — it contains everything."

She was only sixteen, this sharp-witted little girl, and a beautiful blonde. She thought everything of me.

Fantine was one of those women who do wrong in the most virtuous and touching manner. This is a peculiarity of French grisettes.

You are an Englishman, and you don't understand. Learn, my friend, learn. Come to Paris and improve your morals.

Fantine was the soul of modesty. She always wore high-neck dresses. High-neck dresses are a sign of modesty.

Fantine loved Tholmoyes. Why? My God! What are you to do? It was the fault of her parents, and she had n't any. How shall you teach her? You must teach the parent if you wish to educate the child. How would you become virtuous?

Teach your grandmother!

V.

WHEN Tholmoyes ran away from Fantine, — which was done in a charming, gentlemanly manner, — Fantine became convinced that a rigid sense of propriety might look upon her conduct as immoral. She was a creature of sensitiveness, — and her eyes were opened.

She was virtuous still, and resolved to break off the *liaison* at once.

So she put up her wardrobe and baby in a bundle. Child as she was, she loved them both. Then left Paris.

VI.

FANTINE'S native place had changed.

M. Madeline — an angel, and inventor of jet-work — had been teaching the villagers how to make spurious jet.

This is a progressive age. Those Americans, — children of the West, — they make nutmegs out of wood.

I, myself, have seen hams made of pine, in the wigwams of those children of the forest.

But civilization has acquired deception too. Society is made up of deception. Even the best French society.

Still there was one sincere episode.

Eh ?

The French Revolution!

VII.

M. MADELINE was, if anything, better than Myriel.

M. Myriel was a saint. M. Madeline a good man.

M. Myriel was dead. M. Madeline was living.

That made all the difference.

M. Madeline made virtue profitable. I have seen it written : —

" Be virtuous and you will be happy."

Where did I see this written ? In the modern Bible ? No. In the Koran ? No. In Rousseau ? No. Diderot ? No. Where then ?

In a copy-book.

VIII.

M. MADELINE was M. le Maire.

This is how it came about.

For a long time he refused the honor. One day an old woman, standing on the steps, said : —

" Bah, a good mayor is a good thing.

" You are a good thing.

" Be a good mayor."

This woman was a rhetorician. She understood inductive ratiocination.

IX.

WHEN this good M. Madeline, whom the reader will perceive must have been a former convict, and a very bad man, gave himself up to justice as the real Jean Valjean, about this same time, Fantine was turned away from the manufactory, and met with a number of losses from society. Society attacked her, and this is what she lost : —

First her lover.

Then her child.

Then her place.

Then her hair.

Then her teeth.

Then her liberty.

Then her life.

What do you think of society after that? I tell you the present social system is a humbug.

X.

This is necessarily the end of Fantine.

There are other things that will be stated in other volumes to follow. Don't be alarmed; there are plenty of miserable people left.

Au revoir — my friend.

"LA FEMME."

AFTER THE FRENCH OF M. MICHELET.

———◆———

I.

WOMEN AS AN INSTITUTION.

"IF it were not for women, few of us would at present be in existence." This is the remark of a cautious and discreet writer. He was also sagacious and intelligent.

Woman! Look upon her and admire her. Gaze upon her and love her. If she wishes to embrace you, permit her. Remember she is weak and you are strong.

But don't treat her unkindly. Don't make love to another woman before her face, even if she be your wife. Don't do it. Always be polite, even should she fancy somebody better than you.

If your mother, my dear Amadis, had not fancied your father better than somebody, you might

have been that somebody's son. Consider this.
Always be a philosopher, even about women.

Few men understand women. Frenchmen, perhaps, better than any one else. I am a Frenchman.

II.

THE INFANT.

SHE is a child — a little thing — an infant.

She has a mother and father. Let us suppose,
for example, they are married. Let us be moral
if we cannot be happy and free — they are married — perhaps — they love one another — who
knows ?

But she knows nothing of this ; she is an infant
— a small thing — a trifle !

She is not lovely at first. It is cruel, perhaps,
but she is red, and positively ugly. She feels this
keenly and cries. She weeps. Ah, my God, how
she weeps ! Her cries and lamentations now are
really distressing.

Tears stream from her in floods. She feels
deeply and copiously like M. Alphonse de La-
martine in his *Confessions.*

If you are her mother, Madame, you will fancy worms; you will examine her linen for pins, and what not.   Ah, hypocrite! you, even *you*, misunderstand her.

Yet she has charming natural impulses.   See how she tosses her dimpled arms.   She looks longingly at her mother.   She has a language of her own.   She says, "goo goo," and "ga ga."

She demands something — this infant!

She is faint, poor thing.   She famishes.   She wishes to be restored.   Restore her, Mother!

It is the first duty of a mother to restore her child!

III.

THE DOLL.

SHE is hardly able to walk; she already totters under the weight of a doll.

It is a charming and elegant affair.   It has pink cheeks and purple-black hair.   She prefers brunettes, for she has already, with the quick knowledge of a French infant, perceived she is a blonde, and that her doll cannot rival her.   *Mon*

Dieu, how touching ! Happy child ! She spends hours in preparing its toilet. She begins to show her taste in the exquisite details of its dress. She loves it madly, devotedly. She will prefer it to *bonbons*. She already anticipates the wealth of love she will hereafter pour out on her lover, her mother, her father, and finally, perhaps, her husband.

This is the time the anxious parent will guide these first outpourings. She will read her extracts from Michelet's *L'Amour*, Rousseau's *Héloise*, and the *Revue des deux Mondes*.

IV.

THE MUD PIE.

SHE was in tears to-day.

She had stolen away from her *bonne* and was with some rustic infants. They had noses in the air, and large, coarse hands and feet.

They had seated themselves around a pool in the road, and were fashioning fantastic shapes in the clayey soil with their hands. Her throat swelled and her eyes sparkled with delight as, for the first time, her soft palms touched the plastic mud. She made a graceful and lovely pie. She stuffed it with stones for almonds and plums. She forgot everything. It was being baked in the solar rays, when madame came and took her away.

She weeps. It is night, and she is weeping still.

V.

HER FIRST LOVE.

SHE no longer doubts her beauty. She is loved.

She saw him secretly. He is vivacious and sprightly. He is famous. He has already had an affair with Finfin, the *fille de chambre,* and poor Finfin is desolate. He is noble. She knows he is the son of Madame la Baronne Couturière. She adores him.

She affects not to notice him. Poor little thing ! Hippolyte is distracted — annihilated — inconsolable and charming.

She admires his boots, his cravat, his little gloves — his exquisite pantaloons — his coat, and cane.

She offers to run away with him.   He is transported, but magnanimous.   He is wearied, perhaps. She sees him the next day offering flowers to the daughter of Madame la Comtesse Blanchisseuse.

She is again in tears.

She reads *Paul et Virginie.* She is secretly transported.   When she reads how the exemplary young woman laid down her life rather than appear *en déshabillé* to her lover, she weeps again.   Tasteful and virtuous Bernardine de St. Pierre ! — the daughters of France admire you !

All this time her doll is headless in the cabinet. The mud pie is broken on the road.

VI.

THE WIFE.

SHE is tired of loving and she marries.

Her mother thinks it, on the whole, the best thing. As the day approaches, she is found frequently in tears.   Her mother will not permit the affianced one to see her, and he makes several attempts to commit suicide.

But something happens. Perhaps it is winter, and the water is cold. Perhaps there are not enough people present to witness his heroism.

In this way her future husband is spared to her. The ways of Providence are indeed mysterious. At this time her mother will talk with her. She will offer philosophy. She will tell her she was married herself.

But what is this new and ravishing light that breaks upon her? The toilet and wedding clothes! She is in a new sphere.

She makes out her list in her own charming writing. Here it is. Let every mother heed it.*

     *   *   *   *   *

     *   *   *   *   *

She is married. On the day after, she meets her old lover, Hippolyte. He is again transported.

VII.

HER OLD AGE.

A Frenchwoman never grows old.

* The delicate reader will appreciate the omission of certain articles for which English synonymes are forbidden.

MARY McGILLUP.

A SOUTHERN NOVEL.

AFTER BELLE BOYD.

WITH AN INTRODUCTION BY G. A. S—LA.

———◆———

INTRODUCTION.

" WILL you write me up ? "

The scene was near Temple Bar. The speaker was the famous rebel Mary McGillup, — a young girl of fragile frame, and long, lustrous black hair. I must confess that the question was a peculiar one, and, under the circumstances, somewhat puzzling. It was true I had been kindly treated by the Northerners, and, though prejudiced against them, was to some extent under obligations to them. It was true that I knew little or nothing of American politics, history, or geography. But when did an English writer ever weigh such trifles? Turning to the speaker, I inquired with some caution the amount of pecuniary compensation offered for the work.

" Sir ! " she said, drawing her fragile form to its full height, " you insult me, — you insult the South."

"But look ye here, d' ye see — the tin — the blunt — the

ready — the stiff, you know. Don't ye see, we can't do without that, you know ! "

" It shall be contingent on the success of the story," she answered haughtily. " In the mean time take this precious gem." And drawing a diamond ring from her finger, she placed it with a roll of MSS. in my hands and vanished.

Although unable to procure more than £1 2 s. 6 d. from an intelligent pawnbroker to whom I stated the circumstances and with whom I pledged the ring, my sympathies with the cause of a downtrodden and chivalrous people were at once enlisted. I could not help wondering that in rich England, the home of the oppressed and the free, a young and lovely woman like the fair author of those pages should be obliged to thus pawn her jewels — her marriage gift — for the means to procure her bread ! With the exception of the English aristocracy, — who much resemble them, — I do not know of a class of people that I so much admire as the Southern planters. May I become better acquainted with both !

Since writing the above, the news of Mr. Lincoln's assassination has reached me. It is enough for me to say that I am dissatisfied with the result. I do not attempt to excuse the assassin. Yet there will be men who will charge this act upon the chivalrous South. This leads me to repeat a remark once before made by me in this connection, which has become justly celebrated. It is this : —

" It is usual, in cases of murder, to look for the criminal

among those who expect to be benefited by the crime. In the death of Lincoln, his immediate successor in office alone receives the benefit of his dying."

If her Majesty Queen Victoria were assassinated, which Heaven forbid, the one most benefited by her decease would, of course, be his Royal Highness the Prince of Wales, her immediate successor. It would be unnecessary to state that suspicion would at once point to the real culprit, which would of course be his Royal Highness. This is logic.

But I have done. After having thus stated my opinion in favor of the South, I would merely remark that there is One who judgeth all things, — who weigheth the cause between brother and brother, — and awardeth the perfect retribution; and whose ultimate decision I, as a British subject, have only anticipated.

G. A. S.

CHAPTER I.

EVERY reader of Belle Boyd's narrative will remember an allusion to a " lovely, fragile-looking girl of nineteen," who rivalled Belle Boyd in devotion to the Southern cause, and who, like her, earned the enviable distinction of being a " rebel spy."

I am that " fragile " young creature. Although
on friendly terms with the late Miss Boyd, now
Mrs. Hardinge, candor compels me to state that
nothing but our common politics prevents me
from exposing the ungenerous spirit she has displayed in this allusion. To be dismissed in a
single paragraph after years of — But I anticipate.
To put up with this feeble and forced acknowledgment of services rendered would be a confession of a craven spirit, which, thank God, though
"*fragile*" and only "*nineteen*," I do not possess.
I may not have the "*blood of a Howard*" in my
veins, as some people, whom I shall not disgrace
myself by naming, claim to have, but I have yet
to learn that the race of McGillup ever yet brooked
slight or insult.   I shall not say that attention in
certain quarters seems to have turned *some people's*
heads ; nor that it would have been more delicate
if certain folks had kept quiet on the subject of
their courtship, and the rejection of certain offers,
when it is known that their forward conduct
was all that procured them a husband ! Thank
Heaven, the South has some daughters who are
above such base considerations ! While nothing

shall tempt me to reveal the promises to share
equally the fame of certain enterprises, which
were made by one who shall now be nameless, I
have deemed it only just to myself to put my own
adventures upon record. If they are not equal to
those of another individual, it is because, though
"fragile," my education has taught me to have
some consideration for the truth. I am done.

CHAPTER II.

I was born in Missouri. My dislike for the
Northern scum was inherent. This was shown, at
an early age, in the extreme distaste I exhibited
for Webster's spelling-book, — the work of a well-
known Eastern Abolitionist. I cannot be too grateful for the consideration shown by my chivalrous
father, — a gentleman of the old school, — who
resisted to the last an attempt to introduce Mitchell's Astronomy and Geography into the public
school of our district. When I state that this
same Mitchell became afterward a hireling helot
in the Yankee Army, every intelligent reader will

appreciate the prophetic discrimination of this true son of the South.

I was eight years old when I struck the first blow for Southern freedom against the Northern Tyrant. It is hardly necessary to state that in this instance the oppressor was a pale, overworked New England " schoolmarm." The principle for which I was contending, I felt, however, to be the same. Resenting an affront put upon me, I one day heaved a rock* at the head of the Vandal schoolmistress. I was seized and overpowered. My pen falters as I reach the climax. English readers will not give credit to this sickening story, — the civilized world will avert its head, — but I, Mary McGillup, was publicly SPANKED !

CHAPTER III.

BUT the chaotic vortex of civil war approached, and fell destruction, often procrastinated, brooded in storm.† As the English people may like to

* NOTE, BY G. A. S. — In the Southwest, any stone larger than a pea is termed "a rock."

† I make no pretension to fine writing, but perhaps Mrs. Hardinge can lay over that. O, of course !   M. McG.

know what was really the origin of the rebellion, I have no hesitation in giving them the true and only cause. Slavery had nothing to do with it, although the violation of the Declaration of Independence, in the disregard by the North of the Fugitive Slave Law,* might have provoked a less fiery people than the Southrons. At the inception of the struggle a large amount of Southern indebtedness was held by the people of the North. To force payment from the generous but insolvent debtor — to obtain liquidation from the Southern planter — was really the soulless and mercenary object of the craven Northerners. Let the common people of England look to this. Let the improvident literary hack ; the starved impecunious Grub Street debtor ; the newspaper frequenter of sponging-houses, remember this in their criticisms of the vile and slavish Yankee.

* The Declaration of Independence grants to each subject "the pursuit of life, liberty, and happiness." A fugitive slave may be said to personify " life, liberty, and happiness." Hence his pursuit is really legal. This is logic. G. A. S.

CHAPTER IV.

THE roasting of an Abolitionist, by a greatly
infuriated community, was my first taste of the
horrors of civil war. Heavens! Why will the
North persist in this fratricidal warfare? The
expulsion of several Union refugees, which soon
followed, now fairly plunged my beloved State in
the seething vortex.

I was sitting at the piano one afternoon, singing
that stirring refrain, so justly celebrated, but which
a craven spirit, unworthy of England, has excluded
from some of her principal restaurants, and was
dwelling with some enthusiasm on the following
line : —

"Huzza! she spurns the Northern scum!"

when a fragment of that scum, clothed in that
detestable blue uniform which is the symbol of
oppression, entered the apartment. "I have the
honor of addressing the celebrated rebel spy, Miss
McGillup," said the Vandal officer.

In a moment I was perfectly calm. With the

exception of slightly expectorating twice in the
face of the minion, I did not betray my agitation.
Haughtily, yet firmly, I replied : —

" I am."

" You looked as if you might be," the brute
replied, as he turned on his heel to leave the
apartment.

In an instant I threw myself before him. " You
shall not leave here thus," I shrieked, grappling
him with an energy which no one, seeing my frail
figure, would have believed. " I know the reputation of your hireling crew. I read your dreadful
purpose in your eye. Tell me not that your
designs are not sinister. You came here to insult me, — to kiss me, perhaps. You sha' n't, —
you naughty man. Go away ! "

The blush of conscious degradation rose to the
cheek of the Lincoln hireling as he turned his face
away from mine.

In an instant I drew my pistol from my belt,
which, in anticipation of some such outrage, I
always carried, and shot him.

CHAPTER V.

"Thy forte was less to act than speak,
                              Maryland !
Thy politics were changed each week,
                              Maryland !
With Northern Vandals thou wast meek,
With sympathizers thou wouldst shriek,
I know thee — O, 't was like thy cheek !
                    Maryland ! my Maryland !"

AFTER committing the act described in the preceding chapter, which every English reader will
pardon, I went up stairs, put on a clean pair of
stockings, and, placing a rose in my lustrous black
hair, proceeded at once to the camp of Generals
Price and Mosby to put them in possession of information which would lead to the destruction of
a portion of the Federal Army. During a great
part of my flight I was exposed to a running
fire from the Federal pickets of such coarse expressions as, "Go it, Sally Reb," "Dust it, my
Confederate beauty," but I succeeded in reaching
the glorious Southern camp uninjured.

In a week afterwards I was arrested, by a *lettre de cachet* of Mr. Stanton, and placed in the *Bastile*. British readers of my story will express surprise at these terms, but I assure them that not only these articles but *tumbrils, guillotines,* and *conciergeries* were in active use among the Federals. If substantiation be required, I refer to the Charleston *Mercury,* the only reliable organ, next to the New York *Daily News,* published in the country. At the *Bastile* I made the acquaintance of the accomplished and elegant author of *Guy Livingstone,** to whom I presented a curiously carved thigh-bone of a Union officer, and from whom I received the following beautiful acknowledgment : —

" *Demoiselle :* — Should I ever win hame to my ain countrie, I make mine avow to enshrine in my *reliquaire* this elegant *bijouterie* and offering of *La Belle Rebelle.* Nay, methinks this fraction of man's anatomy were some compensation for the rib lost by the ' grand old gardener,' Adam."

* The recent conduct of Mr. Livingstone renders him unworthy of my notice. His disgusting praise of Belle Boyd, and complete ignoring of my claims, show the artfulness of some females and puppyism of some men.   M. McG.

CHAPTER VI.

RELEASED at last from durance vile and placed on board of an Erie canal-boat, on my way to Canada, I for a moment breathed the sweets of liberty. Perhaps the interval gave me opportunity to indulge in certain reveries which I had hitherto sternly dismissed. Henry Breckinridge Folair, a consistent copperhead, captain of the canal-boat, again and again pressed that suit I had so often rejected.

It was a lovely moonlight night. We sat on the deck of the gliding craft. The moonbeam and the lash of the driver fell softly on the flanks of the off horse, and only the surging of the tow-rope broke the silence. Folair's arm clasped my waist. I suffered it to remain. Placing in my lap a small but not ungrateful roll of checkerberry lozenges, he took the occasion to repeat softly in my ear the words of a motto he had just unwrapped — with its graceful covering of the tissue paper — from a sugar almond. The heart of the wicked little rebel, Mary McGillup, was won!

The story of Mary McGillup is done. I might have added the journal of my husband, Henry Breckinridge Folair, but as it refers chiefly to his freights, and a schedule of his passengers, I have been obliged, reluctantly, to suppress it.

It is due to my friends to say that I have been requested not to write this book. Expressions have reached my ears, the reverse of complimentary. I have been told that its publication will probably insure my banishment for life. Be it so. If the cause for which I labored have been subserved, I am content.

London, May, 1865.

THE END.

CONDENSED NOVELS

(Second Series)

NEW BURLESQUES

RUPERT THE RESEMBLER

By A-TH-Y H-PE

CHAPTER I

RUDOLPH OF TRULYRURALANIA

WHEN I state that I was own brother to Lord Burleydon, had an income of two thousand a year, could speak all the polite languages fluently, was a powerful swordsman, a good shot, and could ride anything from an elephant to a clothes-horse, I really think I have said enough to satisfy any feminine novel-reader of Bayswater or South Kensington that I was a hero. My brother's wife, however, did not seem to incline to this belief.

"A more conceited, self-satisfied little cad I never met than you," she said. "Why don't you try to do something instead of sneering at others who do? You never take anything seriously — except yourself, which is n't worth it. You are proud of your red hair and peaked nose just because you fondly believe that you got them from the Prince of Trulyrural-ania, and are willing to think evil of your ancestress to satisfy your snobbish little soul. Let me tell you, sir, that there was no more truth about that than there was in that silly talk of her partiality for her husband's red-haired gamekeeper in Scotland. Ah! that makes you start — don't it? But I have always observed that a mule is apt to remember only the horse side of his ancestry!"

Whenever my pretty sister-in-law talks in this way I always try to forget that she came of a family far inferior to our own, the Razorbills. Indeed, her people — of the Nonconformist stock — really had nothing but wealth and rectitude, and I think my brother Bob, in his genuine love for her, was willing to overlook the latter for the sake of the former.

My pretty sister-in-law's interest in my

affairs always made me believe that she
secretly worshiped me — although it was
a fact, as will be seen in the progress of
this story, that most women blushed on
my addressing them. I used to say it
" was the reflection of my red hair on a
transparent complexion," which was rather
neat — was n't it?   And subtle?   But
then, I was always saying such subtle
things.

" My dear Rose," I said, laying down
my egg spoon (the egg spoon really had
nothing to do with this speech, but it
imparted such a delightfully realistic flavor to the scene), " I 'm not to blame if I
resemble the S'helpburgs."

" It 's your being so beastly proud of
it that I object to! " she replied.   " And
for Heaven's sake, try to *be* something,
and not merely resemble things!   The
fact is you resemble too much — you 're
always resembling.   You resemble a man
of fashion, and you 're not; a wit, and

you 're not ; a soldier, a sportsman, a hero — and you 're none of 'em. Altogether, you 're not in the least convincing. Now, listen ! There 's a good chance for you to go as our *attaché* with Lord Mumblepeg, the new Ambassador to Cochin China. In all the novels, you know, *attachés* are always the confidants of Grand Duchesses, and know more state secrets than their chiefs ; in real life, I believe they are something like a city clerk with a leaning to private theatricals. Say you 'll go ! Do ! "

" I 'll take a few months' holiday first," I replied, " and then," I added in my gay, dashing way, " if the place is open — hang it if I don't go ! "

" Good old bounder ! " she said, " and don't think too much of that precious Prince Rupert. He was a bad lot."

She blushed again at me — as her husband entered.

" Take Rose's advice, Rupert, my boy," he said, " and go ! "

And that is how I came to go to Truly-ruralania. For I secretly resolved to take my holiday in traveling in that country and trying, as dear Lady Burleydon put it, really to be somebody, instead of resembling anybody in particular. A precious lot *she* knew about it!

CHAPTER II

IN WHICH MY HAIR CAUSES A LOT OF THINGS

You go to Trulyruralania from Charing Cross. In passing through Paris we picked up Mlle. Beljambe, who was going to Köhlslau, the capital of Trulyruralania, to marry the Grand Duke Michael, who, however, as I was informed, was in love with the Princess Flirtia. She blushed on seeing me — but, I was told afterwards, declined being introduced to me on any account. However, I thought nothing of this, and went on to Bock, the next station to Köhlslau. At the little inn in the forest I was informed I was just in time to see the coronation of the new king the next day. The landlady and her daughter were very communicative, and, after the fashion of the simple, guileless stage peasant, instantly informed me what everybody was doing, and at once explained the situation. She told me that the Grand Duke Michael — or Black Michael as he was called — himself aspired to the throne, as well as to the hand of the Princess Flirtia, but was hated by the populace, who preferred the young heir, Prince Rupert; because he had the hair and features of the dynasty of the S'helpburgs, " which," she added, " are singularly like your own."

" But is red hair so very peculiar here?" I asked.

" Among the Jews — yes, sire ! I mean yes, *sir*," she corrected herself. " You seldom see a red-headed Jew."

" The Jews!" I repeated in astonishment.

" Of course you know the S'helpburgs are descended directly from Solomon — and have indeed some of his matrimonial peculiarities," she said, blushing.

I was amazed — but recalled myself. "But why do they call the Duke of Köhlslau *Black Michael?*" I asked carelessly.

"Because he is nearly black, sir. You see, when the great Prince Rupert went abroad in the old time he visited England, Scotland, and Africa. They say he married an African lady there — and that the Duke is really more in the direct line of succession than Prince Rupert."

But here the daughter showed me to my room. She blushed, of course, and apologized for not bringing a candle, as she thought my hair was sufficiently illuminating. "But," she added with another blush, "I do *so* like it."

I replied by giving her something of no value, — a Belgian nickel which would n't pass in Bock, as I had found to my cost. But my hair had evidently attracted attention from others, for on my return to the guest-room a stranger ap-

proached me, and in the purest and most
precise German — the Court or 'Olland
Hof speech — addressed me :

"Have you the red hair of the fair
King or the hair of your father ? "

Luckily I was able to reply with the
same purity and precision : " I have both
the hair of the fair King and my own.
But I have not the hair of my father nor
of Black Michael, nor of the innkeeper
nor the innkeeper's wife. The red *heir*
of the fair King would be a son."

Possibly this delicate *mot* on the approaching marriage of the King was lost
in the translation, for the stranger strode
abruptly away. I learned, however, that
the King was actually then in Bock, at
the castle a few miles distant, in the
woods. I resolved to stroll thither.

It was a fine old mediæval structure.
But as the singular incidents I am about
to relate combine the romantic and adventurous atmosphere of the middle ages

with all the appliances of modern times, I
may briefly state that the castle was lit by
electricity, had fire-escapes on each of the
turrets, four lifts, and was fitted up by
one of the best West End establishments.
The sanitary arrangements were excellent,
and the drainage of the most perfect order,
as I had reason to know personally later.
I was so affected by the peaceful solitude
that I lay down under a tree and presently
fell asleep. I was awakened by the sound
of voices, and, looking up, beheld two men
bending over me. One was a grizzled
veteran, and the other a younger dandy-
fied man ; both were dressed in shooting
suits.

" Never saw such a resemblance before
in all my life," said the elder man. " 'Pon
my soul ! if the King had n't got shaved
yesterday because the Princess Flirtia
said his beard tickled her, I 'd swear it
was he ! "

I could not help thinking how lucky

it was — for this narrative — that the
King *had* shaved, otherwise my story
would have degenerated into a mere Com-
edy of Errors.   Opening my eyes, I said
boldly :

" Now that you are satisfied who I resemble, gentlemen, perhaps you will tell
me who you are ? "

" Certainly," said the elder curtly.   " I
am Spitz — a simple colonel of his Majesty's, yet, nevertheless, the one man who
runs this whole dynasty — and this young
gentleman is Fritz, my lieutenant.   And
you are ——— ? "

" My name is Razorbill — brother to
Lord Burleydon," I replied calmly.

" Good heavens ! another of the lot ! "
he muttered.   Then, correcting himself,
he said brusquely : " Any relation to that
Englishwoman who was so sweet on the
old Rupert centuries ago ? "

Here, again, I suppose my sister-in-law
would have had me knock down the foreign

insulter of my English ancestress — but I colored to the roots of my hair, and even farther — with pleasure at this proof of my royal descent! And then a cheery voice was heard calling "Spitz!" and "Fritz!" through the woods.

"The King!" said Spitz to Fritz quickly. "He must not see him."

"Too late," said Fritz, as a young man bounded lightly out of the bushes.

I was thunderstruck! It was as if I had suddenly been confronted with a mirror — and beheld myself! Of course he was not quite so good-looking, or so tall, but he was still a colorable imitation! I was delighted.

Nevertheless, for a moment he did not seem to reciprocate my feeling. He stared at me, staggered back and passed his hand across his forehead. "Can it be," he muttered thickly, "that I've got 'em agin? Yet I only had — shingle glash!"

But Fritz quickly interposed.

" Your Majesty is all right — though,"
he added in a lower voice, " let this be a
warning to you for to-morrow ! This
gentleman is Mr. Razorbill — you know
the old story of the Razorbills ? — Ha!
ha ! "

But the King did not laugh ; he extended his hand and said gently, " You
are welcome — my cousin ! " Indeed,
my sister-in-law would have probably said
that — dissipated though he was — he
was the only gentleman there.

" I have come to see the coronation,
your Majesty," I said.

" And you shall," said the King heartily, " and shall go with us ! The show
can't begin without us — eh, Spitz?" he
added playfully, poking the veteran in the
ribs, " whatever Michael may do ! "

Then he linked his arms in Spitz's and
mine. " Let 's go to the hut — and have
some supper and fizz," he said gayly.

We went to the hut. We had supper.

We ate and drank heavily. We danced madly around the table. Nevertheless I thought that Spitz and Fritz were worried by the King's potations, and Spitz at last went so far as to remind his Majesty that they were to start early in the morning for Köhlslau. I noticed also that as the King drank his speech grew thicker and Spitz and Fritz exchanged glances. At last Spitz said with stern significance :

" Your Majesty has not forgotten the test invariably submitted to the King at his coronation ? "

"Shertenly not," replied the King, with his reckless laugh. " The King mush be able to pronounsh — name of his country — intel-lillil-gibly : mush shay (hic !) : ' I 'm King of — King of — Too-too-tooral-looral-anyer.' " He staggered, laughed, and fell under the table.

" He cannot say it ! " gasped Fritz and Spitz in one voice. " He is lost ! "

" Unless," said Fritz suddenly, pointing

at me with a flash of intelligence, " *he* can personate him, and say it. Can you?" he turned to me brusquely.

It was an awful moment. I had been drinking heavily too, but I resolved to succeed. " I 'm King of Trooly-rooly —— " I murmured; but I could not master it — I staggered and followed the King under the table.

" Is there no one here," roared Spitz, " who can shave thish dynasty, and shay ' Tooral—— '? No! —— it! I mean ' Trularlooral—— ' " but he, too, lurched hopelessly forward.

" No one can say ' Tooral-looral—— ' " muttered Fritz; and, grasping Spitz in despair, they both rolled under the table.

How long we lay there, Heaven knows! I was awakened by Spitz playing the garden hose on me. He was booted and spurred, with Fritz by his side. The King was lying on a bench, saying feebly: " Blesh you, my chillen."

" By politely acceding to Black Michael's request to ' try our one-and-six sherry,' he has been brought to this condition," said Spitz bitterly. " It 's a trick to keep him from being crowned. In this country if the King is crowned while drunk, the kingdom instantly reverts to a villain — no matter who. But in this case the villain is Black Michael. Ha ! What say you, lad ? Shall we frustrate the rascal, by having *you* personate the King ? "

I was — well ! — intoxicated at the thought ! But what would my sister-in-law say ? Would she — in her Nonconformist conscience — consider it strictly honorable ? But I swept all scruples aside. A King was to be saved ! " I will go," I said. " Let us on to Köhlslau — riding like the wind ! " We rode like the wind, furiously, madly. Mounted on a wild, dashing bay — known familiarly as the " Bay of Biscay " from its rough turbulence — I easily kept the lead. But our horses began to fail. Suddenly Spitz halted, clapped his hand to his head, and threw himself from his horse. " Fools! " he said, " we should have taken the train ! It will get there an hour before we will ! " He pointed to a wayside station where the 7.15 excursion train for Köhlslau was waiting.

" But how dreadfully unmediæval ! — What will the public say ? " I began.

" Bother the public ! " he said gruffly. " Who's running this dynasty — you or I ? Come ! " With the assistance of Fritz he tied up my face with a handkerchief to simulate toothache, and then, with a shout of defiance, we three rushed madly into a closely packed third-class carriage.

Never shall I forget the perils, the fatigue, the hopes and fears of that mad journey. Panting, perspiring, packed together with cheap trippers, but exalted with the one hope of saving the King, we at last staggered out on the Köhlslau platform utterly exhausted. As we did so we heard a distant roar from the city. Fritz turned an ashen gray, Spitz a livid blue. "Are we too late?" he gasped, as we madly fought our way into the street, where shouts of "The King! The King!" were rending the air. "Can it be Black Michael?" But here the crowd parted, and a procession, preceded by outriders, flashed into the square. And there, seated in a carriage beside the most beautiful red-haired girl I had ever seen, was the King, — the King whom we had left two hours ago, dead drunk in the hut in the forest!

CHAPTERS III TO XXII (Inclusive)

IN WHICH THINGS GET MIXED

WE reeled against each other aghast! Spitz recovered himself first. " We must fly ! " he said hoarsely. " If the King has discovered our trick — we are lost ! "

" But where shall we go ? " I asked.

" Back to the hut."

We caught the next train to Bock. An hour later we stood panting within the hut. Its walls and ceiling were splashed with sinister red stains. " Blood ! " I exclaimed joyfully. " At last we have a real mediæval adventure ! "

" It's Burgundy, you fool," growled Spitz ; " good Burgundy wasted ! " At this moment Fritz appeared dragging in the hut-keeper.

" Where is the King ? " demanded

Spitz fiercely of the trembling peasant.

"He was carried away an hour ago by Black Michael and taken to the castle."

"And when did he *leave* the castle?" roared Spitz.

"He never left the castle, sir, and, alas! I fear never will, alive!" replied the man, shuddering.

We stared at each other! Spitz bit his grizzled mustache. "So," he said bitterly, "Black Michael has simply anticipated us with the same game! We have been tricked. I knew it could not be the King whom they crowned! No!" he added quickly, "I see it all — it was Rupert of Glasgow!"

"Who is Rupert of Glasgow?" I cried.

"Oh, I really can't go over all that family rot again," grunted Spitz. "Tell him, Fritz."

Then, taking me aside, Fritz delicately informed me that Rupert of Glasgow —

a young Scotchman — claimed equally
with myself descent from the old Rupert,
and that equally with myself he resembled
the King.   That Michael had got possession of him on his arrival in the country,
kept him closely guarded in the castle,
and had hid his resemblance in a black
wig and false mustache ; that the young
Scotchman, however, seemed apparently
devoted to Michael and his plots ; and
there was undoubtedly some secret un-
derstanding between them.   That it was
evidently Michael's trick to have the pretender crowned, and then, by exposing
the fraud and the condition of the real
King, excite the indignation of the duped
people, and seat himself on the throne !
" But," I burst out, " shall this base-born
pretender remain at Köhlslau beside the
beautiful Princess Flirtia ?   Let us to
Köhlslau at once and hurl him from the
throne ! "

" One pretender is as good as another,"

said Spitz dryly. "But leave *him* to me.
'T is the King we must protect and succor! As for that Scotch springald, before
midnight I shall have him kidnaped,
brought back to his master in a close carriage, and you — *you* shall take his place
at Köhlslau."

"I will," I said enthusiastically, drawing my sword; "but I have done nothing
yet. Please let me kill something!"

"Aye, lad!" said Spitz, with a grim
smile at my enthusiasm. "There's a
sheep in your path. Go out and cleave it
to the saddle. And bring the saddle
home!"

My sister-in-law might have thought
me cruel — but I did it.

CHAP XXIII AND SOME OTHER CHAPS

I KNOW not how it was compassed, but that night Rupert of Glasgow was left bound and gagged against the door of the castle, and the night-bell pulled. And that night I was seated on the throne of the S'helpburgs. As I gazed at the Princess Flirtia, glowing in the characteristic beauty of the S'helpburgs, and admired her striking profile, I murmured softly and half audibly: "Her nose is as a tower that looketh toward Damascus."

She looked puzzled, and knitted her pretty brows. "Is that poetry?" she asked.

"No," I said promptly. "It's only part of a song of our great Ancestor." As she blushed slightly, I playfully flung around her fair neck the jeweled collar

of the Order of the S'helpburgs — three
golden spheres pendant, quartered from
the arms of Lombardy — with the ancient
Syric motto, *El Ess Dee*.

She toyed with it a moment, and then
said softly: "You have changed, Rupert.
Do ye no ken hoo?"

I looked at her — as surprised at her
dialect as at the imputation.

"You don't talk that way, as you did.
And you don't say, 'It *will* be twelve
o'clock,' when you mean, 'It *is* twelve
o'clock,' nor 'I will be going out,' when
you mean 'I *am*.' And you didn't say,
'Eh, sirs!' or 'Eh, mon,' to any of the
Court — nor 'Hoot awa!' nor any of
those things. And," she added with a
divine little pout, "you haven't told me
I was 'sonsie' or 'bonnie' once."

I could with difficulty restrain myself.
Rage, indignation, and jealousy filled my
heart almost to bursting. I understood
it all; that rascally Scotchman had made

the most of his time, and dared to get ahead of me! I did not mind being taken for the King, but to be confounded with this infernal descendant of a gamekeeper — was too much! Yet with a superhuman effort I remained calm — and even smiled.

"You are not well?" said the Princess earnestly. "I thought you were taking too much of the Strasbourg pie at supper! And you are not going, surely — so soon?" she added, as I rose.

"I must go at once," I said. "I have forgotten some important business at Bock."

"Not boar hunting again?" she said poutingly.

"No, I'm hunting a red dear," I said with that playful subtlety which would make her take it as a personal compliment, though I was only thinking of that impostor, and longing to get at him, as I bowed and withdrew.

In another hour I was before Black

Michael's castle at Bock.   These are lightning changes, I know — and the sover-
eignty of Trulyruralania *was* somewhat
itinerant — but when a kingdom and a
beautiful Princess are at stake, what are
you to do ?   Fritz had begged me to take
him along, but I arranged that he should
come later, and go up unostentatiously in
the lift.   I was going by way of the moat.
I was to succor the King, but I fear my
real object was to get at Rupert of Glasgow.

I had noticed the day before that a
large outside drain pipe, decreed by the
Bock County Council, ran from the moat
to the third floor of the donjon keep.   I
surmised that the King was imprisoned on
that floor.   Examining the pipe closely, I
saw that it was really a pneumatic dispatch
tube, for secretly conveying letters and
dispatches from the castle through the
moat beyond the castle walls.   Its extraordinary size, however, gave me the hor-

rible conviction that it was to be used to convey the dead body of the King to the moat. I grew cold with horror — but I was determined.

I crept up the pipe. As I expected, it opened funnel-wise into a room where the poor King was playing poker with Black Michael. It took me but a moment to dash through the window into the room, push the King aside, gag and bind Black Michael, and lower him by a stout rope into the pipe he had destined for another. Having him in my power, I lowered him until I heard his body splash in the water in the lower part of the pipe. Then I proceeded to draw him up again, intending to question him in regard to Rupert of Glasgow. But this was difficult, as his saturated clothing made him fit the smooth pipe closely. At last I had him partly up, when I was amazed at a rush of water from the pipe which flooded the room. I dropped him and pulled him up again

with the same result. Then in a flash I
saw it all. His body, acting like a pis-
ton in the pipe, had converted it into a
powerful pump. Mad with joy, I rapidly
lowered and pulled him up again and
again, until the castle was flooded — and
the moat completely drained ! I had created the diversion I wished ; the tenants
of the castle were disorganized and bewildered in trying to escape from the
deluge, and the moat was accessible to
my friends. Placing the poor King on a
table to be out of the water, and tying
up his head in my handkerchief to disguise him from Michael's guards, I drew
my sword and plunged downstairs with
the cataract in search of the miscreant
Rupert. I reached the drawbridge, when
I heard the sounds of tumult and was
twice fired at, — once, as I have since
learned, by my friends, under the impression that I was the escaping Rupert of
Glasgow, and once by Black Michael's

myrmidons, under the belief that I was
the King. I was struck by the fact that
these resemblances were confusing and
unfortunate! At this moment, however,
I caught sight of a kilted figure leaping
from a lower window into the moat. Some
instinct impelled me to follow it. It rapidly crossed the moat and plunged into
the forest, with me in pursuit. I gained
upon it; suddenly it turned, and I found
myself again confronted with *myself* —
and apparently the King! But that very
resemblance made me recognize the Scotch
pretender, Rupert of Glasgow. Yet he
would have been called a " braw laddie,"
and his handsome face showed a laughing
good humor, even while he opposed me,
claymore in hand.

"Bide a wee, Maister Rupert Razorbill,"
he said lightly, lowering his sword, " before we slit ane anither's weasands. I 'm
no claimin' any descent frae kings, and
I 'm no acceptin' any auld wife's clavers

against my women forbears, as ye are!
I 'm just paid gude honest siller by Black
Michael for the using of ma face and figure — sic time as his Majesty is tae worse
frae trink! And I 'm commeesioned frae
Michael to ask ye what price *ye* would
take to join me in performing these duties
— turn and turn aboot. Eh, laddie —
but he would pay ye mair than that daft
beggar, Spitz."

Rage and disgust overpowered me.
" And *this* is my answer," I said, rushing
upon him.

I have said earlier in these pages that
I was a " strong " swordsman. In point
of fact, I had carefully studied in the
transpontine theatres that form of melo-
dramatic mediæval sword-play known as
"two up and two down." To my disgust,
however, this wretched Scotchman did not
seem to understand it, but in a twinkling
sent my sword flying over my head. Before I could recover it, he had mounted a

horse ready saddled in the wood, and, shouting to me that he would take my "compleements" to the Princess, galloped away. Even then I would have pursued him afoot, but, hearing shouts behind me, I turned as Spitz and Fritz rode up.

"Has the King escaped to Köhlslau?" asked Fritz, staring at me.

"No," I said, "but Rupert of Glasgow" —

"—— Rupert of Glasgow," growled Spitz. "We've settled him! He's gagged and bound and is now on his way to the frontier in a close carriage."

"Rupert — on his way to the frontier?" I gasped.

"Yes. Two of my men found him, disguised with a handkerchief over his face, trying to escape from the castle. And while we were looking for the King, whom we supposed was with you, they have sent the rascally Scotchman home."

"Fool!" I gasped. "Rupert of Glas-

gow has just left me! *You have deported
your own King.*" And overcome by my
superhuman exertions, I sank unconscious
to the ground.

When I came to, I found myself in a
wagon lit, speeding beyond the Trulyruralania frontier. On my berth was lying
a missive with the seal of the S'helpburgs.
Tearing it open I recognized the handwriting of the Princess Flirtia.

MY DEAR RUPERT, — Owing to the
confusion that arises from there being so
many of you, I have concluded to accept
the hand of the Duke Michael. I may
not become a Queen, but I shall bring
rest to my country, and Michael assures
me in his playful manner that "three of
a kind," "even of the same color," do not
always win at poker. It will tranquilize
you somewhat to know that the Lord
Chancellor assures me that on examining
the records of the dynasty he finds that

my ancestor Rupert never left his kingdom during his entire reign, and that consequently your ancestress has been grossly maligned. I am sending typewritten copies of this to Rupert of Glasgow and the King. Farewell.

FLIRTIA.

Once a year, at Christmastide, I receive a simple foreign hamper *via* Charing Cross, marked " Return empty." I take it in silence to my own room, and there, opening it, I find — unseen by any other eyes but my own — a modest *pâté de foie gras*, of the kind I ate with the Princess Flirtia. I take out the *pâté*, replace the label, and have the hamper reconveyed to Charing Cross.

THE STOLEN CIGAR CASE

By A. CO-N D-LE

THE STOLEN CIGAR CASE

I FOUND Hemlock Jones in the old
Brook Street lodgings, musing before the
fire. With the freedom of an old friend
I at once threw myself in my usual familiar attitude at his feet, and gently
caressed his boot. I was induced to do
this for two reasons : one, that it enabled me to get a good look at his bent,
concentrated face, and the other, that it
seemed to indicate my reverence for his
superhuman insight. So absorbed was
he even then, in tracking some mysterious
clue, that he did not seem to notice me.
But therein I was wrong — as I always
was in my attempt to understand that
powerful intellect.

" It is raining," he said, without lifting
his head.

" You have been out, then?" I said quickly.

" No.   But I see that your umbrella is wet, and that your overcoat has drops of water on it."

I sat aghast at his penetration.   After a pause he said carelessly, as if dismissing the subject : " Besides, I hear the rain on the window.   Listen."

I listened.   I could scarcely credit my ears, but there was the soft pattering of drops on the panes.   It was evident there was no deceiving this man !

" Have you been busy lately?" 1 asked, changing the subject.   " What new problem — given up by Scotland Yard as inscrutable — has occupied that gigantic intellect ? "

He drew back his foot slightly, and seemed to hesitate ere he returned it to its original position.   Then he answered wearily : " Mere trifles — nothing to speak of.   The Prince Kupoli has been

here to get my advice regarding the disappearance of certain rubies from the
Kremlin; the Rajah of Pootibad, after
vainly beheading his entire bodyguard,
has been obliged to seek my assistance to
recover a jeweled sword.   The Grand
Duchess of Pretzel-Brauntswig is desirous
of discovering where her husband was
on the night of February 14; and last
night " — he lowered his voice slightly
— " a lodger in this very house, meeting
me on the stairs, wanted to know why
they did n't answer his bell."

I could not help smiling — until I saw
a frown gathering on his inscrutable forehead.

" Pray remember," he said coldly,
" that it was through such an apparently
trivial question that I found out Why
Paul Ferroll Killed His Wife, and What
Happened to Jones ! "

I became dumb at once.   He paused
for a moment, and then suddenly chang-

ing back to his usual pitiless, analytical
style, he said: "When I say these are
trifles, they are so in comparison to an
affair that is now before me. A crime
has been committed, — and, singularly
enough, against myself. You start," he
said. "You wonder who would have
dared to attempt it. So did I; nevertheless, it has been done. *I* have been
robbed ! "

"*You* robbed ! You, Hemlock Jones,
the Terror of Peculators ! " I gasped in
amazement, arising and gripping the table
as I faced him.

"Yes ! Listen. I would confess it to
no other. But *you* who have followed
my career, who know my methods; you,
for whom I have partly lifted the veil
that conceals my plans from ordinary
humanity, — you, who have for years
rapturously accepted my confidences, passionately admired my inductions and in-
ferences, placed yourself at my beck and

call, become my slave, groveled at my feet, given up your practice except those few unremunerative and rapidly decreasing patients to whom, in moments of abstraction over *my* problems, you have administered strychnine for quinine and arsenic for Epsom salts; you, who have sacrificed anything and everybody to me, — *you* I make my confidant!"

I arose and embraced him warmly, yet he was already so engrossed in thought that at the same moment he mechanically placed his hand upon his watch chain as if to consult the time. "Sit down," he said. "Have a cigar?"

"I have given up cigar smoking," I said.

"Why?" he asked.

I hesitated, and perhaps colored. I had really given it up because, with my diminished practice, it was too expensive. I could afford only a pipe. "I prefer a pipe," I said laughingly. "But tell me of this robbery. What have you lost?"

He arose, and planting himself before the fire with his hands under his coat-tails, looked down upon me reflectively for a moment. "Do you remember the cigar case presented to me by the Turkish Ambassador for discovering the missing favorite of the Grand Vizier in the fifth chorus girl at the Hilarity Theatre? It was that one. I mean the cigar case. It was incrusted with diamonds."

"And the largest one had been supplanted by paste," I said.

"Ah," he said, with a reflective smile, "you know that?"

"You told me yourself. I remember considering it a proof of your extraordinary perception. But, by Jove, you don't mean to say you have lost it?"

He was silent for a moment. "No; it has been stolen, it is true, but I shall still find it. And by myself alone! In your profession, my dear fellow, when a member is seriously ill, he does not prescribe for himself, but calls in a brother doctor. Therein we differ. I shall take this matter in my own hands."

" And where could you find better ? " I said enthusiastically. " I should say the cigar case is as good as recovered already."

" I shall remind you of that again," he said lightly. " And now, to show you my confidence in your judgment, in spite of my determination to pursue this alone, I am willing to listen to any suggestions from you."

He drew a memorandum book from his pocket and, with a grave smile, took up his pencil.

I could scarcely believe my senses. He, the great Hemlock Jones, accepting suggestions from a humble individual like myself! I kissed his hand reverently, and began in a joyous tone :

" First, I should advertise, offering a reward ; I should give the same intimation in hand-bills, distributed at the ' pubs ' and the pastry-cooks'. I should next visit the different pawnbrokers ; I should give notice at the police station. I should examine the servants. I should thoroughly search the house and my own pockets. I speak relatively," I added, with a laugh. " Of course I mean *your* own."

He gravely made an entry of these details.

" Perhaps," I added, " you have already done this ? "

" Perhaps," he returned enigmatically. " Now, my dear friend," he continued, putting the note-book in his pocket and rising, " would you excuse me for a few moments ? Make yourself perfectly at home until I return ; there may be some things," he added with a sweep of his hand toward his heterogeneously filled shelves, " that may interest you and while away the time. There are pipes and tobacco in that corner."

Then nodding to me with the same inscrutable face he left the room. I was too well accustomed to his methods to think much of his unceremonious withdrawal, and made no doubt he was off to investigate some clue which had suddenly occurred to his active intelligence.

Left to myself I cast a cursory glance over his shelves. There were a number of small glass jars containing earthy substances, labeled "Pavement and Road Sweepings," from the principal thoroughfares and suburbs of London, with the sub-directions "for identifying foot-tracks." There were several other jars, labeled "Fluff from Omnibus and Road Car Seats," "Cocoanut Fibre and Rope Strands from Mattings in Public Places," "Cigarette Stumps and Match Ends from Floor of Palace Theatre, Row A, 1 to 50." Everywhere were evidences of this wonderful man's system and perspicacity.

I was thus engaged when I heard the

slight creaking of a door, and I looked up
as a stranger entered. He was a rough-
looking man, with a shabby overcoat and
a still more disreputable muffler around
his throat and the lower part of his face.
Considerably annoyed at his intrusion, I
turned upon him rather sharply, when,
with a mumbled, growling apology for
mistaking the room, he shuffled out again
and closed the door. I followed him
quickly to the landing and saw that he
disappeared down the stairs. With my
mind full of the robbery, the incident
made a singular impression upon me. I
knew my friend's habit of hasty absences
from his room in his moments of deep
inspiration ; it was only too probable that,
with his powerful intellect and magnificent
perceptive genius concentrated on one
subject, he should be careless of his own
belongings, and no doubt even forget to
take the ordinary precaution of locking
up his drawers. I tried one or two and

found that I was right, although for some reason I was unable to open one to its fullest extent. The handles were sticky, as if some one had opened them with dirty fingers. Knowing Hemlock's fastidious cleanliness, I resolved to inform him of this circumstance, but I forgot it, alas! until — but I am anticipating my story.

His absence was strangely prolonged. I at last seated myself by the fire, and lulled by warmth and the patter of the rain on the window, I fell asleep. I may have dreamt, for during my sleep I had a vague semi-consciousness as of hands being softly pressed on my pockets — no doubt induced by the story of the robbery. When I came fully to my senses, I found Hemlock Jones sitting on the other side of the hearth, his deeply concentrated gaze fixed on the fire.

"I found you so comfortably asleep that I could not bear to awaken you," he said, with a smile.

I rubbed my eyes. " And what news ? " I asked. " How have you succeeded ? "

" Better than I expected," he said, " and I think," he added, tapping his note-book, " I owe much to *you*."

Deeply gratified, I awaited more. But in vain. I ought to have remembered that in his moods Hemlock Jones was reticence itself. I told him simply of the strange intrusion, but he only laughed.

Later, when I arose to go, he looked at me playfully. " If you were a married man," he said, " I would advise you not to go home until you had brushed your sleeve. There are a few short brown sealskin hairs on the inner side of your forearm, just where they would have adhered if your arm had encircled a seal-skin coat with some pressure ! "

" For once you are at fault," I said triumphantly ; " the hair is my own, as you will perceive ; I have just had it cut at the hairdresser's, and no doubt this arm projected beyond the apron."

He frowned slightly, yet, nevertheless, on my turning to go he embraced me warmly — a rare exhibition in that man of ice. He even helped me on with my overcoat and pulled out and smoothed down the flaps of my pockets. He was particular, too, in fitting my arm in my overcoat sleeve, shaking the sleeve down from the armhole to the cuff with his deft fingers. "Come again soon!" he said, clapping me on the back.

"At any and all times," I said enthusiastically; "I only ask ten minutes twice a day to eat a crust at my office, and four hours' sleep at night, and the rest of my time is devoted to you always, as you know."

"It is indeed," he said, with his impenetrable smile.

Nevertheless, I did not find him at home when I next called. One afternoon, when nearing my own home, I met him in one of his favorite disguises, — a long blue

swallow-tailed coat, striped cotton trousers,
large turn-over collar, blacked face, and
white hat, carrying a tambourine. Of
course to others the disguise was perfect,
although it was known to myself, and I
passed him — according to an old under-
standing between us — without the slight-
est recognition, trusting to a later explanation.   At another time, as I was making
a professional visit to the wife of a pub-
lican at the East End, I saw him, in the
disguise of a broken-down artisan, looking
into the window of an adjacent pawnshop.
I was delighted to see that he was evidently following my suggestions, and in
my joy I ventured to tip him a wink; it
was abstractedly returned.

Two days later I received a note ap-
pointing a meeting at his lodgings that
night.   That meeting, alas! was the one
memorable occurrence of my life, and the
last meeting I ever had with Hemlock
Jones!   I will try to set it down calmly,

though my pulses still throb with the re-
collection of it.

I found him standing before the fire,
with that look upon his face which I had
seen only once or twice in our acquaintance — a look which I may call an absolute concatenation of inductive and deductive ratiocination — from which all that
was human, tender, or sympathetic was
absolutely discharged. He was simply an
icy algebraic symbol ! Indeed, his whole
being was concentrated to that extent that
his clothes fitted loosely, and his head was
absolutely so much reduced in size by his
mental compression that his hat tipped
back from his forehead and literally hung
on his massive ears.

After I had entered he locked the doors,
fastened the windows, and even placed a
chair before the chimney. As I watched
these significant precautions with absorb-
ing interest, he suddenly drew a revolver
and, presenting it to my temple, said in
low, icy tones :

" Hand over that cigar case ! "

Even in my bewilderment my reply was truthful, spontaneous, and involuntary. " I have n't got it," I said.

He smiled bitterly, and threw down his revolver. " I expected that reply! Then let me now confront you with something more awful, more deadly, more relentless and convincing than that mere ethal weapon, — the damning inductive and deductive proofs of your guilt ! " He drew from his pocket a roll of paper and a note-book.

" But surely," I gasped, " you are joking! You could not for a moment believe " —

" Silence ! Sit down ! " I obeyed.

" You have condemned yourself," he went on pitilessly. " Condemned yourself on my processes, — processes familiar to you, applauded by you, accepted by you for years ! We will go back to the time when you first saw the cigar case. Your expressions," he said in cold, deliberate tones, consulting his paper, were, ' How beautiful! I wish it were mine.' This was your first step in crime — and my first indication. From ' I *wish* it were mine' to ' I *will* have it mine,' and the mere detail, ' *How can* I make it mine?' the advance was obvious. Silence! But as in my methods it was necessary that there should be an overwhelming inducement to the crime, that unholy admiration of yours for the mere trinket itself was not enough. You are a smoker of cigars."

" But," I burst out passionately, " I told you I had given up smoking cigars."

" Fool!" he said coldly, " that is the *second* time you have committed yourself. Of course you told me! What more natural than for you to blazon forth that prepared and unsolicited statement to *prevent* accusation. Yet, as I said before, even that wretched attempt to cover up your tracks was not enough. I still had

to find that overwhelming, impelling motive necessary to affect a man like you.
That motive I found in the strongest of
all impulses — Love, I suppose you would
call it," he added bitterly, " that night
you called ! You had brought the most
conclusive proofs of it on your sleeve."

" But — " I almost screamed.

" Silence ! " he thundered. " I know
what you would say. You would say
that even if you had embraced some
Young Person in a sealskin coat, what
had that to do with the robbery? Let me
tell you, then, that that sealskin coat represented the quality and character of your
fatal entanglement ! You bartered your
honor for it — that stolen cigar case was
the purchaser of the sealskin coat !

" Silence ! Having thoroughly estab-
lished your motive, I now proceed to the
commission of the crime itself. Ordinary
people would have begun with that —
with an attempt to discover the where-

abouts of the missing object. These are not *my* methods."

So overpowering was his penetration that, although I knew myself innocent, I licked my lips with avidity to hear the further details of this lucid exposition of my crime.

" You committed that theft the night I showed you the cigar case, and after I had carelessly thrown it in that drawer. You were sitting in that chair, and I had arisen to take something from that shelf. In that instant you secured your booty without rising. Silence! Do you remember when I helped you on with your overcoat the other night? I was particular about fitting your arm in. While doing so I measured your arm with a spring tape measure, from the shoulder to the cuff. A later visit to your tailor confirmed that measurement. It proved to be *the exact distance between your chair and that drawer !*"

I sat stunned.

"The rest are mere corroborative details! You were again tampering with the drawer when I discovered you doing so! Do not start! The stranger that blundered into the room with a muffler on — was myself! More, I had placed a little soap on the drawer handles when I purposely left you alone. The soap was on your hand when I shook it at parting. I softly felt your pockets, when you were asleep, for further developments. I embraced you when you left — that I might feel if you had the cigar case or any other articles hidden on your body. This confirmed me in the belief that you had already disposed of it in the manner and for the purpose I have shown you. As I still believed you capable of remorse and confession, I twice allowed you to see I was on your track: once in the garb of an itinerant negro minstrel, and the second time as a workman looking in the window of the pawnshop where you pledged your booty."

"But," I burst out, "if you had asked the pawnbroker, you would have seen how unjust" —

"Fool!" he hissed, "that was one of *your* suggestions — to search the pawn-shops! Do you suppose I followed any of your suggestions, the suggestions of the thief? On the contrary, they told me what to avoid."

"And I suppose," I said bitterly, "you have not even searched your drawer?"

"No," he said calmly.

I was for the first time really vexed. I went to the nearest drawer and pulled it out sharply. It stuck as it had before, leaving a part of the drawer unopened. By working it, however, I discovered that it was impeded by some obstacle that had slipped to the upper part of the drawer, and held it firmly fast. Insert-ing my hand, I pulled out the impeding object. It was the missing cigar case! I turned to him with a cry of joy.

But I was appalled at his expression. A look of contempt was now added to his acute, penetrating gaze. " I have been mistaken," he said slowly ; " I had not allowed for your weakness and cowardice! I thought too highly of you even in your guilt! But I see now why you tampered with that drawer the other night. By some inexplicable means — possibly another theft — you took the cigar case out of pawn and, like a whipped hound, restored it to me in this feeble, clumsy fashion. You thought to deceive me, Hemlock Jones! More, you thought to destroy my infallibility. Go! I give you your liberty. I shall not summon the three policemen who wait in the adjoining room — but out of my sight forever ! "

As I stood once more dazed and petrified, he took me firmly by the ear and

led me into the hall, closing the door behind him. This reopened presently, wide
enough to permit him to thrust out my
hat, overcoat, umbrella, and overshoes,
and then closed against me forever!

I never saw him again. I am bound
to say, however, that thereafter my business increased, I recovered much of my
old practice, and a few of my patients
recovered also. I became rich. I had a
brougham and a house in the West End.
But I often wondered, pondering on that
wonderful man's penetration and insight,
if, in some lapse of consciousness, I had
not really stolen his cigar case!

GOLLY AND THE CHRISTIAN,

OR

THE MINX AND THE MANXMAN

By H-LL C-NE

BOOK I

GOLLY COYLE was the only granddaughter of a vague and somewhat simple clergyman who existed, with an aunt, solely for Golly's epistolary purposes. There was, of course, intermediate ancestry, — notably a dead mother who was French, and therefore responsible for any later naughtiness in Golly, — but they have no purpose here. They lived in the Isle of Man. Golly knew a good deal of Man, for even at the age of twelve she was in love with John Gale — only son of Lord Gale, who was connected with the Tempests. Gales, however, were frequent and remarkable along the coast, so that it was not singular that one day she found John "coming on" on a headland where she was sitting. His dog had "pointed" her. "It's exceedingly impolite to point to anything you want," said Golly. Touched by this, and overcome by a strange emotion, John Gale turned away and went to Canada. Slight as the incident was, it showed that inborn chivalry to women, that desire for the Perfect Life, that intense eagerness to incarnate Christianity in modern society, which afterward distinguished him. Golly loved him! For all that, she still remained a "tomboy" as she was, — robbing orchards, mimicking tramps and policemen, buttering the stairs and the steps of houses, tying kettles to dogs' tails, and marching in a white jersey, with the curate's hat on, through the streets of the village. "Gol dern my skin!" said the dear old clergyman, as he tried to emerge from a surplice which Golly had stitched together; "what spirits the child *do* have!" Yet everybody loved her! And when John Gale returned from Canada, and looked into her big blue eyes one day at church, small wonder that he immediately went off again to Paris, and an extended Continental sojourn, with a serious leaning to theology! Golly bore his absence meekly but characteristically; got a boat, disported like a duck in the water, attempted to elope with a boy appropriately named Drake, but encountered a half gale at sea and a whole Gale in John on a yacht, who rescued them both. Convinced now that there was but one way to escape from his Fate — Golly! — John Gale took holy orders and at once started for London. As he stood on the deck of the steamer he heard an imbecile chuckle in his ear. It was the simple old clergyman: "You are going to London to join the Church, John; Golly is going there, too, as hospital nurse. There's a pair of you! He! he! Look after her, John, and protect her Manx simplicity." Before John could recover himself, Golly was

at his side executing the final steps of a
"cellar-door flap jig" to the light-hearted
refrain : —

" We are a simple family — we are — we are —we are ! "

And even as her pure young voice
arose above the screams of the departure
whistle, she threw a double back-somer-
sault on the quarter-deck, cleverly alighting on the spikes of the wheel before the
delighted captain.

" Jingle my electric bells," he said,
looking at the bright young thing, " but
you 're a regular minx " —

" I beg your pardon," interrupted John
Gale, with a quick flush.

" I mean a regular *Manx*," said the
captain hurriedly.

A singular paleness crossed the deeply
religious face of John. As the vessel rose
on the waves, he passed his hand hurriedly first across his brows and then over
his high-buttoned clerical waistcoat, that

visible sign of a devoted ascetic life!
Then murmuring in his low, deep voice,
" Brandy, steward," he disappeared be-
low.

BOOK II

GLORIOUS as were Golly's spirits, exquisitely simple her worldly ignorance, and irresistible her powers of mimicry, strangely enough they were considered out of place in St. Barabbas' Hospital. A light-hearted disposition to mistake a blister for a poultice; that rare Manx conscientiousness which made her give double doses to the patients as a compensation when she had omitted to give them a single one, and the faculty of bursting into song at the bedside of a dying patient, produced some liveliness not unmixed with perplexity among the hospital staff. It is true, however, that her performance of clog-dancing during the night-watches drew a larger and more persistent attendance of students and young surgeons than

ever was seen before. Yet everybody
loved her! Even her patients! "If it
amooses you, miss, to make me tyke the
pills wot's meant for the lydy in the next
ward, I ain't complyning," said an East
End newsboy. "When ye tyke off the
style of the doctor wot wisits me, miss,
and imitates his wyes, Lawd! it does me
as much good as his mixtures," said a
consumptive charwoman. Even thus, old
and young basked in the radiant youth
of Golly. She found time to write to her
family : —

DEAR OLD PALS! I'm here. J'y suis!
bet your boots! While you're wondering
what has become of the Bright Young
Thing, the B. Y. T. is lookin' out of
the winder of St. Barabbas' Hospital —
just taking in all of dear, roaring, dirty
London in one gulp! Such a place —
Lordy! I've been waiting three hours
to see the crowd go by, and they have n't

gone yet! Such crowds, such busses, —
all green and blue, only a penny fare,
and you can ride on top if you want to!
Think of that, you dear old Manx people!
But there — " the bell goes a-ringing for
Sarah ! " — they 're calling for Nurse !
That 's the worst of this job : they 're
always a-dyin' just as you 're getting
interested in something else ! Ta-ta !

GOLLY !

Then her dear old grandfather wrote :

I 'm wondering where my diddleums,
Golly, is ! We all miss you so much,
deary, though we don't miss so many
little things as when you were here. My
dear, conscientious, unselfish little girl !
You don't say where John Gale is. Is
he still protecting you — he-he ! — you
giddy, naughty thing ! People wonder
on the island why I let you go alone to
London — they forget your dear mother

was a Frenchwoman! If you see anything your dear old grandfather would like — send it on. GRANFER.

Later, her aunt wrote : —

Have you seen the Queen yet, and does she wear her crown at breakfast? You might get over the area railing at Buckingham Palace — it would be nothing for a girl like you to do — and see if you can find out.

To these letters Golly answered, in her own light-hearted way : —

DEAR GRANKINS, — I have n't seen John much — but I think he 's like the Private Secretary at the play — he "don't like London." Lordy! there — I 've let it out! I 've been to a theayter. Nurse Jinny Jones and me scrouged into the pit one night without paying, " pertendin',"

as we were in uniform, we had come
to take out a " Lydy " that had fainted.
Such larks! and such a glorious theayter!
I 'll tell you another time. Tell aunty
the Queen 's always out when I call. But
that 's nothing, everybody else is so affa-
ble and polite in London. Gentlemen —
" real toffs," they call 'em — whom you
don't know from Adam — think nothing
of speaking to you in the street. Why,
Nurse Jinny says — but there another
patient 's going off who by rights oughter
have died only to-morrow. " To-morrow
and to-morrow and to-morrow," as that
barn-stormer actor said. But they 're
always calling for that giddy young thing,

Your   GOLLY.

Meantime, John Gale, having abruptly
left Golly at the door of St. Barabbas'
Hospital, tactfully avoiding an unseemly
altercation with the cab-driver regarding
her exact fare, pursued his way thought-

fully to the residence of his uncle, the
First Lord of the Admiralty. He found
his Lordship in his bath-room. He was
leaning over the bath-tub, which was half
full of water, contemplating with some
anxiety the model of a line-of-battle ship
which was floating on it, bottom upward.
" I don't think it can be quite right — do
you ? " he said, nervously grasping his
nephew's hand as he pointed to the cap-
sized vessel ; " yet they always do it. Tell
me ! " he went on appealingly, " tell me,
as a professing Christian and a Perfect
Man — is it quite right ? "

" I should think, sir," responded John
Gale, with uncompromising truthfulness,
" that the average vessel of commerce is
not built in that way."

" Yet," said the First Lord of the Admiralty, with a far-off look, " they all do
it ! And they don't steer ! The larger
they are and the more recent the model,
the less they steer. Dear me — you ought

to see 'em go round and round in that tub." Then, apparently recalling the probable purpose of John's visit, he led the way into his dressing-room. "So you are in London, dear boy. Is there any little thing you want? I have," he continued, absently fumbling in the drawers of his dressing-table, "a few curacies and a bishopric somewhere, but with these blessed models — I can't think where they are. Or what would you say to a nice chaplaincy in the navy, with a becoming uniform, on one of those thingummies?" He pointed to the bath-room. "Stay," he continued, as he passed his hand over his perplexed brows, "now I think of it — you're quite unorthodox! Dear me! that would n't do. You see, Drake," — he paused, as John Gale started, — "I mean Sir Francis Drake, once suspended his chaplain for unorthodoxy, according to Froude's book. These admirals are dreadfully strict Churchmen. No matter!

Come again some other time," he added, gently pushing his nephew downstairs and into the street, " and we 'll see about it."

With a sinking heart, John turned his steps toward Westminster. He would go and see Golly ; perhaps he had not looked after her as he ought. Suddenly a re-membered voice, in mimicking accents, fell upon his ear with the quotation, " Do you know ? "   Then, in a hansom passing swiftly by him, Golly, in hospital dress with flying ribbons, appeared, sitting be-tween Lord Brownstone Ewer and Francis Horatio Nelson Drake, completely grown up. And from behind floated the inex-pressibly sad refrain, " Hi tiddli hi ! "

This is how it happened. One morn-ing, Jinny Jones, another hospital nurse, had said to her, " Have you any objec-tion, dear, to seeing a friend of another gent, a friend of mine ? "

" None in the least, dear," said Golly. " I want to see all that can be seen, and

10—v. 5

do all that can be done in London, and
know the glory thereof. I only require
that I shall be allowed to love John Gale
whenever he permits it, which is n't often,
and that I may be permitted to write
simple letters to my doting relations at
the rate of twelve pages a day, giving
an account — *my own* account — of my
doings. There! Go on now! Bring on
your bears."

They had visited the chambers which
Lord Brownstone and Drake occupied
together, and in girlish innocence had put
on the gentlemen's clothes and danced
before them. Then they all went to the
theatre, where Golly's delightful simplicity
and childish ignorance of the world had
charmed them. Everything to her was
new, strange, and thrilling. She even
leaned from the carriage windows to see
the "wheels go round." She was surprised at the number of people in the
theatre, and insisted on knowing if it was

church, because they all sat there in their best clothes so quietly. She believed that the play was real, and frequently, from a stage box, interrupted the acting with explanations. She informed the heroine of the design of the villain waiting at the wings. And when the aged mother of the heroine was dying of starvation in a hovel, and she threw a bag of bonbons on the stage, with the vociferous declaration that "Lord Brownstone had just given them to her — but — Lordy ! — *she* did n't want them," they were obliged to lead her away, closely followed by an usher and a policeman. "To think," she wrote to John Gale, "that the audience only laughed and shouted, and never offered to help ! And yet look at the churches in London, where they dare to preach the gospel ! "

Fired by this simple letter, and alarmed by Golly's simplicity, John Gale went to his clerical chief, Archdeacon Luxury, and demanded permission to preach next Sunday. " Certainly," said the Archdeacon ; " you shall take my curate's place. I shall inform the congregation that you are the son of Lord Gale. They are very particular churchmen — all society people — and of course will be satisfied with the work of the Lord, especially," he added, with a polite smile, " when that work happens to be — the Lord Gale's son." Accordingly, the next Sunday, John Gale occupied the pulpit of St. Swithin. But an unexpected event happened. His pent-up eagerness to denounce the present methods of Christianity, his fullness of utterance, defeated his purpose. He was overcome with a kind of pulpit fright. His ideas of time and place fled him. After beginning, " Mr. Chairman, in rising to propose the toast of our worthy Archdeacon — Fellow Manxmen — the present moment — er — er — the proudest in my — er

— life — Dearly beloved Golly — unaccustomed as I am to public speaking," he abruptly delivered the benediction and sat down. The incident, however, provoked little attention. The congregation, accustomed to sleep through the sermon, awoke at the usual time and went home. Only a single Scotchwoman said to him in passing : "Verra weel for a beginning, laddie. But give it hotter to 'em next time." Discomfited and bewildered, he communed with himself gloomily. "I can't marry Golly. I can't talk. I hate society. What 's to be done? I have it! I 'll go into a monastery."

He went into a monastery in Bishopsgate Street, reached by a threepenny 'bus. He gave out vaguely that he had got into " Something Good, in the City." Society was satisfied. Only Golly suspected the truth. She wrote to her grandfather : —

" I saw John Gale the other day with

a crowd following him in the Strand.
He had on only a kind of brown serge
dressing-gown, tied around his waist by a
rope, and a hood on his head. I think
his poor ' toe-toes ' were in sandals, and
I dare say his legs were cold, poor dear.
However, if he calls *that* protection of
Golly — *I* don't ! I might be run off at
any moment — for all he 'd help. No
matter ! If this Court understands herself, and she thinks she do, Golly can
take care of herself — you bet."

Nevertheless, Golly lost her place at
the hospital through her heroic defense
of her friend Jinny Jones, who had been
deceived by Lord Brownstone Ewer.
" You would drive that poor girl into the
street," she said furiously to the Chairman
of the Board, throwing her cap and apron
in their faces. " You 're a lot of rotten
old hypocrites, and I 'm glad to get shut of
you." Not content with that, she went
to Drake and demanded that he should

make his friend Lord Brownstone marry Jinny.

"Sorry — awfully sorry — my dear Golly, but he 's engaged to a rich American girl who is to pay his debts; but I 'll see that he does something handsome for Jinny. And *you*, my child, what are *you* going to do without a situation?" he added, with touching sympathy. "You see, I 've some vague idea of marrying you myself," he concluded meditatively.

"Thank you for nothing," interrupted Golly gayly, "but I can take care of myself and follow out my mission like John Gale."

"There 's a pair of you, certainly," said Drake, with a tinge of jealous bitterness.

"You bet it 's 'a pair' that will take your 'two knaves,' you and your Lord Brownstone," returned Golly, dropping a mock courtesy. "Ta-ta; I 'm going on the stage."

BOOK III

She went first into a tobacconist's —
and sold cigarettes. Sometimes she suffered from actual want, and ate fried fish.
" Do you know how nice fried fish tastes
in London, — you on ' the Oilan' ? " she
wrote gayly. " I 'm getting on splendidly; so 's John Gale, I suppose, though
he 's looking cadaverous from starving
himself all round. Tell aunty I have n't
seen the Queen yet, though after all I
really believe she has not seen me."

Then, after a severe struggle, she succeeded in getting on the stage as a song
and dance girl. She sang melodiously
and danced divinely, so remarkably that
the ignorant public, knowing her to be a
Manx girl, and vaguely associating her
with the symbol of the Isle of Man, sup-

posed she had three legs. She was the success of the season; her cup of ambition was filled. It was slightly embittered by the news that her friend Jinny Jones had killed herself in the church at the wedding of her recreant lover and the American heiress. But the affair was scarcely alluded to by the Society papers — who were naturally shocked at the bad taste of the deceased. And even Golly forgot it all — on the stage.

BOOK IV

MEANWHILE John Gale, or Brother
Boreas, as he was known in the monastery, was submitting — among other rig-
ors — to an exceptionally severe winter
in Bishopsgate Street, which seemed to
have an Arctic climate of its own, — possibly induced by the " freezing-out " pro-
cess of certain stock companies in its
vicinity.

" You are miserable, and eager to get
out in the wicked world again, my son,"
said the delightful old Superior, as he sat
by the only fire, sipping a glass of mulled
port, when John came in from shoveling
snow outside. " I, therefore, merely to
try you, shall make you gatekeeper. The
keys of the monastery front door are
under the door-mat in my cell, but I am

.a sound sleeper." He smiled seraphically, and winked casually as he sipped his port. "We will call it, if you please — a penance."

John threw himself in an agony of remorse and shame at the feet of the Superior. "It is n't of myself I 'm thinking," he confessed wildly, "but of that poor young man, Brother Bones, in the next cell to mine. He is a living skeleton, has got only one lung and an atrophied brain. A night out might do him good."

The Father Superior frowned. "Do you know who he is?"

"No."

"His real name is Jones. Why do you start? You have heard it before?"

John had started, thinking of Jinny Jones, Golly's deserted and self-immolated friend.

"It is an uncommon name," he stammered — "for a monastery, I mean."

"He is or was an uncommon man!" said the Superior gravely. "But," he added resignedly, "we cannot pick and choose our company here. Most of us have done something and have our own reasons for this retreat. Brother Polygamus escaped here from the persecutions of his sixth wife. Even I," continued the Superior with a gentle smile, putting his feet comfortably on the mantelpiece, "have had my little fling, and the dear boys used to say — ahem! — but this is mere worldly vanity. You alone, my dear son," he went on with slight severity, "seem to be wanting in some criminality, or — shall I say? — some appropriate besetting sin to qualify you for this holy retreat. An absolutely gratuitous and blameless idiocy appears to be your only peculiarity, and for this you must do penance. From this day henceforth, I make you doorkeeper! Go on with your shoveling at present, and shut the door behind you;

there's a terrible draught in these corridors."

For three days John Gale underwent an agony of doubt and determination, and it still snowed in Bishopsgate Street.

On the fourth evening he went to Brother Bones.

" Would you like to have an evening out ?"

" I would," said Brother Bones.

" What would you do ?"

" I would go to see my remaining sister." His left eyelid trembled slowly in his cadaverous face.

" But if you should hear she was ruined like the other ? What would you do ?"

A shudder passed over the man. " I have not got my little knife," he said vacantly.

True, he had not! The Brotherhood had no pockets, — or rather only a corporate one, which belonged to the Superior. John Gale lifted his eyes in sublime exaltation. "You shall go out," he said with decision. "Muffle up until you are well out of Bishopsgate Street, where it still snows."

"But how did you get the keys?" said Brother Bones.

"From under the Father Superior's door-mat."

"But that was wrong, Brother."

"The mat bore the inscription, ' Salve,' which you know in Latin means ' Welcome,' " returned John Gale. "It was logically a permission."

The two men gazed at each other silently. A shudder passed over the two left eyelids of their wan spiritual faces.

"But I have no money," said Brother Bones.

"Nor have I. But here is a 'bus ticket and a free pass to the Gaiety. You will probably find Golly somewhere about. Tell her," he said in a hollow voice, "that I 'm getting on."

"I will," said Brother Bones, with a deep cough.

The gate opened and he disappeared in the falling snow. The bloodhound kept by the monastery — one of the real Bishopsgate breed — bayed twice, and licked its huge jaws in ghastly anticipation. "I wonder," said John Gale as he resumed his shoveling, "if I have done exactly right. Candor compels me to admit that it is an open question."

BOOK V

EARLY the next morning, Brother Bones was brought home by Policeman X, his hat crushed, his face haggard, his voice husky and unintelligible. He only said vaguely, "Washertime?"

"It is," said John Gale timidly, in explanation to Policeman X, "a case of spiritual exhaustion following a vigil."

"That warn't her name," said Policeman X sternly. "But don't let this 'ere 'appen again."

John Gale turned to Brother Bones. "Then you saw her — Golly?"

"No," said Brother Bones.

"Why? What on earth have you been doing?"

"Dunno! Found myself in stashun — zis morning! Thashall!"

Then John Gale sought the Superior in an agony of remorse, and confessed all. " I am unfit to remain doorkeeper. Remove me," he groaned bitterly.

The old man smiled gently. " On the contrary, I should have given you the keys myself. Hereafter you can keep them. The ways of our Brotherhood are mysterious, — indeed, you may think idiotic, — but we are not responsible for them. It's all Brother Caine's doing — it's 'All Caine ! "

BOOK VI

NEVERTHELESS, John Gale left the monastery. "The Bishopsgate Street winter does not suit me," he briefly explained to the Superior. "I must go south or southwest."

But he did neither. He saw Golly, who was living west. He upbraided her for going on the stage. She retorted: "Whose life is the more artificial, yours or mine? It is true that we are both imperfectly clothed," she added, glancing at a photograph of herself in a short skirt, "and not always in our right mind — but you've caught nothing but a cold! Nevertheless, I love you and you love me."

Then he begged her to go with him to the South Seas and take the place of Father Damien among the colony of lepers.

" It is a beautiful place, and inexpensive, for we shall live only a few weeks. What do you say, dearest ? You know," he added, with a faint, sad smile, glancing at another photograph of her, — executing the high kick, — " you 're quite a leaper yourself."

But that night she received an offer of a new engagement. She wrote to John Gale : " The South Seas is rather an expensive trip to take simply to die. Could n't we do it as cheaply at home ? Or could n't you prevail on your Father Superior to set up his monastery there ? I 'm afraid I 'm not up to it. Why don't you try the old ' Oilan,' nearer home ? There 's lots of measles and diphtheria about there lately."

When the heartbroken John Gale received this epistle, he also received a letter from his uncle, the First Lord of the Admiralty. " I don't fancy this Damien whim of yours. If you 're really in earnest about killing yourself, why not take a brief trial trip in one of our latest iron-clads? It's just as risky, although — as we are obliged to keep these things quiet in the Office — you will not of course get that publicity your noble soul craves."

Abandoned by all in his noble purposes, John Gale took the first steamer to the Isle of Man.

BOOK VII

But he did not remain there long. Once back in that epistolary island, he wrote interminable letters to Golly. When they began to bore each other, he returned to London and entered the Salvation Army. Crowds flocked to hear him preach. He inveighed against Society and Wickedness as represented in his mind by Golly and her friends, and praised a perfect Christianity represented by himself and *his* friends. A panic of the same remarkable character as the Bishopsgate Street winter took possession of London. Old Moore's, Zadkiel's, and Mother Shipton's prophecies were to be fulfilled at an early and fixed date, with no postponement on account of weather. Suddenly Society, John Drake, and Antichrist generally combined by ousting him from his church, and turning it into a music-hall for Golly! Then John Gale took his last and sublime resolve. His duty as a perfect Christian was to kill Golly! His logic was at once inscrutable, perfect, and — John Galish!

With this sublime and lofty purpose, he called upon Golly. The heroic girl saw his purpose in his eye — an eye at once black, murderous, and Christian-like. For an instant she thought it was better to succumb at once and thus end this remarkable attachment. Suddenly through this chaos of Spiritual, Religious, Ecstatic, Super-Egotistic whirl of confused thought, darted a gleam of Common, Ordinary Horse Sense! John Gale saw it illumine her blue eyes, and trembled. God in Mercy! If it came to *that!*

"Sit down, John," she said calmly. Then, in her sweet, clear voice, she said: "Did it ever occur to you, dearest, that a

more ridiculous, unconvincing, purpose-
less, insane, God-forsaken idiot than you
never existed ?   That you eclipse the
wildest dreams of insanity ?   That you
are a mental and moral ' What-is-it ? ' "

" It has occurred to me," he replied
simply.   " I began life with vast asinine
possibilities which fall to the lot of few
men ; yet I cannot say that I have carried even *them* to a logical conclusion !
But *you,* love ! *you,* darling ! conceived
in extravagance, born to impossibility, a
challenge to credulity, a problem to the
intellect, a ' missing word ' for all ages,
— are you aware of any one as utterly
unsympathetic, unreal, and untrue to nature as you are, existing on the face of
the earth, or in the waters under the
earth ? "

" You are right, dearest ; there are
none," she returned with the same calm,
level voice.   " It is true that I have at
times tried to do something real and wo-

manly, and not, you know, merely to com-
plicate a — a "— her voice faltered —
" theatrical situation — but I could n't !
Something impelled me otherwise.   Now
you know why I became an actress !   But
even there I fail !   *They* are allowed
reasoning power off the stage — I have
none at any time !   I laugh in the wrong
place — I do the unnecessary, extravagant thing.   Endowed by some strange
power with extraordinary attributes, I am
supposed to make everybody love me, but
I don't — I satisfy nobody ; I convince
none !   I have no idea what will happen
to me next.   I am doomed to — I know
not what."

" And I," he groaned bitterly, " I, in
some rare and lucid moments, have had a
glimpse of this too.   We are in the hands
of some inscrutable but awful power.   Tell
me, Golly, tell me, darling, who is it ? "

Again that gleam of Common or Ordinary Horse Sense came in her eye.

"I have found out who," she whispered. "I have found out who has created us, and made us as puppets in his hands."

"Is it the Almighty?" he asked.

"No; it is"—she said, with a burst of real laughter—"it is—The 'All Caine!"

"What! our countryman the Manxman? The only great Novelist? The beloved of Gladstone?" he gasped.

"Yes—and he intends to kill *you*—and we're only to be married at your deathbed!"

John Gale arose with a look of stern determination. "I have suffered much and idiotically—but I draw a line at this. I shall kick!"

Golly clapped her hands joyfully. "We will!"

"And we'll chuck him."

"We will."

They were choking with laughter.

"And go and get married in a natural, simple way like anybody else — and try — to do our duty — to God — to each other — and to our fellow-beings — and quit this — damned — nonsense — and in-fer-nal idiocy forever!"

"Amen!"

PUBLISHER'S NOTE. — "In that supreme work of my life, 'The Christian,'" said the gifted novelist to a reporter in speaking of his methods, "I had endowed the characters of Golly and John Gale with such superhuman vitality and absolute reality that — as is well known in the experience of great writers — they became thinking beings, and actually criticised my work, and even *interfered* and *rebelled* to the point of altering my climax and the end!" The present edition gives that ending, which of course is the only real one.

THE ADVENTURES OF JOHN LONGBOWE, YEOMAN

BEING A MODERN-ANTIQUE REALISTIC ROMANCE

(COMPILED FROM SEVERAL EMINENT SOURCES)

THE ADVENTURES OF JOHN LONGBOWE, YEOMAN

It seemeth but fair that I, John Longbowe, should set down this account of
such hap and adventure as hath befallen
me, without flourish, vaporing, or cozen-
ing of speech, but as becometh one who,
not being a ready writer, goeth straight
to the matter in hand in few words. So,
though I offend some, I shall yet convince
all, the which lieth closer to my purpose.
Thus, it was in the year 1560, or 1650,
or mayhap 1710 — for my memory is
not what it hath been and I ever cared
little for monkish calendars or such dry-
as-dust matter, being active as becometh
one who hath to make his way in the
world — yet I wot well it was after the
Great Plague, which I have great cause

to remember, lying at my cozen's in Wardour Street, London, in that lamentable year, eating of gilly flowers, sulphur, hartes tongue and many stynking herbes; touching neither man nor mayd, save with a great tongs steept in pitch; wearing a fine maske of silk with a mouth piece of aromatic stuff — by reason of which acts of hardihood and courage I was miraculously preserved. This much I shall say as to the time of these happenings, and no more. I am a plain, blunt man — mayhap rude of speech should occasion warrant — so let them who require the exactness of a scrivener or a pedagogue go elsewhere for their entertainment and be hanged to them !

Howbeit, though no scholar, I am not one of those who misuse the English speech, and, being foolishly led by the hasty custom of scriveners and printers to write the letters " T " and " H " joined together, which resembleth a " Y," do incontinently jump to the conclusion the THE is pronounced " Ye," — the like of which I never heard in all England. And though this be little toward those great enterprises and happenings I shall presently shew, I set it down for the behoof of such malapert wights as must needs gird at a man of spirit and action — and yet, in sooth, know not their own letters.

So to my tale. There was a great frost when my Lord bade me follow him to the water gate near our lodgings in the Strand. When we reached it we were amazed to see that the Thames was frozen over and many citizens disporting themselves on the ice — the like of which no man had seen before. There were fires built thereon, and many ships and barges were stuck hard and fast, and my Lord thought it vastly pretty that the people were walking under their bows and cabbin windows and climbing of their sides like mermen, but I, being a plain, blunt man, had no joy

in such idlenesse, deeming it better that
in these times of pith and enterprise they
should be more seemly employed. My
Lord, because of one or two misadventures
by reason of the slipperiness of the ice,
was fain to go by London Bridge, which
we did; my Lord as suited his humor
ruffling the staid citizens as he passed or
peering under the hoods of their wives
and daughters — as became a young gallant of the time. I, being a plain, blunt
man, assisted in no such folly, but contented myself, when they complayned to
me, with damning their souls for greasy
interfering varlets. For I shall now make
no scruple in declaring that my Lord was
the most noble Earl of Southampton, being withheld from so saying before through
very plainness and bluntness, desiring as
a simple yeoman to make no boast of
serving a man of so high quality.

We fared on over Bankside to the
Globe playhouse, where my Lord bade me

dismount and deliver a secret message to the chief player — which message was, " had he diligently perused and examined that he wot of, and what said he thereof?" Which I did. Thereupon he that was called the chief player did incontinently proceed to load mine arms and wallet with many and divers rolls of manuscripts in my Lord's own hand, and bade me say unto him that there was a great frost over London, but that if he were to perform those plays and masques publickly, there would be a greater frost there — to wit, in the Globe playhouse. This I did deliver with the Manuscripts to my Lord, who changed countenance mightily at the sight of them, but could make nought of the message. At which the lad who held the horses before the playhouse — one Will Shakespeare — split with laughter. Whereat my Lord cursed him for a deer-stealing, coney-catching Warwickshire lout, and cuffed him soundly. I wot there will be those who remember that this Will Shakespeare afterwards became a player and did write plays — which were acceptable even to the Queen's Majesty's self — and I set this down not from vanity to shew I have held converse with such, nor to give a seemingness and colour to my story, but to shew what ill-judged, misinformed knaves were they who did afterwards attribute friendship between my Lord and this Will Shakespeare, even to the saying that he made sonnets to my Lord. Howbeit, my Lord was exceeding wroth, and I, to beguile him, did propose that we should leave our horses and cargoes of manuscript behind and cross on the ice afoot, which conceit pleased him mightily. In sooth it chanced well with what followed, for hardly were we on the river when we saw a great crowd coming from Westminster, before a caravan of strange animals and savages in masks, capering and capricolling, dragging after them divers

sledges quaintly fashioned like swannes,
in which were ladies attired as fairies and
goddesses and such like heathen and wan-
ton trumpery, which I, as a plain, blunt
man, would have fallen to cursing, had
not my Lord himself damned me under
his breath to hold my peace, for that he
had recognized my Lord of Leicester's
colours and that he made no doubt they
were of the Court.   As forsooth this did
presently appear ; also that one of the
ladies was her Gracious Majesty's self —
masked to the general eye, the better to
enjoy these miscalled festivities. I say miscalled, for, though a loyal subject of her
Majesty, and one who hath borne arms at
Tilbury Fort in defence of her Majesty,
it inflamed my choler, as a plain and
blunt man, that her Mightiness should so
degrade her dignity.   Howbeit, as a man
who hath his way to make in the world, I
kept mine eyes well upon the anticks of the
Great, while my Lord joined the group of

maskers and their follies. I recognized
her Majesty's presence by her discourse in
three languages to as many Ambassadors
that were present — though I marked well
that she had not forgotten her own tongue,
calling one of her ladies "a sluttish wench,"
nor her English spirit in cuffing my Lord
of Essex's ears for some indecorum —
which, as a plain man myself, curt in
speech and action, did rejoice me greatly.
But I must relate one feat, the like of
which I never saw in England before or
since. There was a dance of the maskers,
and in the midst of it her Majesty asked
the Ambassador from Spayne if he had
seen the latest French dance. He replied
that he had not. Whereupon Her Most
Excellent Majesty skipt back a pace and
forward a pace, and lifting her hoop, delivered a kick at his Excellency's hat which
sent it flying the space of a good English
ell above his head! Howbeit so great
was the acclamation that her Majesty was

graciously moved to repeat it to my Lord
of Leicester, but, tripping back, her high
heels caught in her farthingale, and she
would have fallen on the ice, but for that
my Lord, with exceeding swiftness and
dexterity, whisked his cloak from his
shoulder, spreading it under her, and so
received her body in its folds on the ice,
without himself touching her Majesty's
person.   Her Majesty was greatly pleased
at this, and bade my Lord buy another
cloak at her cost, though it swallowed an
estate ; but my Lord replyed, after the lying fashion of the time, that it was honour
enough for him to be permitted to keep it
after " it had received her Royal person."
I know that this hap hath been partly
related of another person — the shipman
Raleigh — but I tell such as deny me
that they lie in their teeth, for I, John
Longbowe, have cause — miserable cause
enough, I warrant — to remember it, and
my Lord can bear me out !   For, spite of

his fair speeches, when he was quit of the
Royal presence, he threw me his wet and
bedraggled cloak and bade me change it
with him for mine own, which was dry and
warm. And it was this simple act which
wrought the lamentable and cruel deed of
which I was the victim, for, as I followed
my Lord, thus apparelled, across the ice, I
was suddenly set upon and seized, a choke-
pear clapt into my mouth so that I could
not cry aloud, mine eyes bandaged, mine
elbows pinioned at my side in that fatall
cloak like to a trussed fowl, and so I was
carried to where the ice was broken, and
thrust into a boat. Thence I was conveyed in the same rude sort to a ship,
dragged up her smooth, wet side, and
clapt under hatches. Here I lay helpless
as in a swoon. When I came to, it was
with a great trampling on the decks above
and the washing of waves below, and I
made that the ship was moving — but
where I knew not. After a little space

the hatch was lifted from where I lay, the choke-pear taken from my mouth ; but not the bandage from mine eyes, so I could see nought around me. But I heard a strange voice say : " What coil is this ? This is my Lord's cloak in sooth, but not my Lord that lieth in it ! Who is this fellow ? " At which I did naturally discover the great misprise of those varlets who had taken me for my dear Lord, whom I now damned in my heart for changing of the cloaks ! Howbeit, when I had fetched my breath with difficulty, being well nigh spent by reason of the gag, I replyed that I was John Longbowe, my Lord's true yeoman, as good a man as any, as they should presently discover when they set me ashore. That I knew — " Softly, friend," said the Voice, " thou knowest too much for the good of England and too little for thine own needs. Thou shalt be sent where thou mayest forget the one and improve thy knowledge of the other." Then as if turning to those about him, for I could not see by reason of the blindfold, he next said : " Take him on your voyage, and see that he escape not till ye are quit of England." And with that they clapt to the hatch again, and I heard him cast off from the ship's side. There was I, John Longbowe, an English yeoman, — I, who but that day had held converse with Will Shakespeare and been cognizant of the revels of Her Most Christian Majesty even to the spying of her garter ! — I was kidnapped at the age of forty-five or thereabout — for I will not be certain of the year — and forced to sea for that my Lord of Southampton had provoked the jealousie and envy of divers other great nobles.

CHAPTERS I TO XX

I AM FORCED TO SEA AND TO BECOME A
PIRATE! I SUFFER LAMENTABLY FROM
SICKNESS BY REASON OF THE BIGNESSE
OF THE WAVES. I COMMIT MANY CRU-
ELTIES AND BLOODSHED. BUT BY THE
DIVINE INTERCESSION I EVENTUALLY
THROW THE WICKED CAPTAIN OVER-
BOARD AND AM ELECTED IN HIS STEAD.
I DISCOVER AN ISLAND OF TREASURE,
OBTAIN POSSESSION THEREOF BY A
TRICKE, AND PUT THE NATIVES TO THE
SWORD

I MARVEL much at those who deem it
necessary in the setting down of their
adventures to gloze over the whiles between with much matter of the country,
the peoples, and even their own foolish
reflections thereon, hoping in this way to

cozen the reader with a belief in their own
truthfulness, and encrease the extravagance of their deeds. I, being a plain,
blunt man, shall simply say for myself
that for many days after being taken
from the bilboes and made free of the
deck, I was grievously distempered by
reason of the waves, and so collapsed in
the bowels that I could neither eat, stand,
nor lie. Being thus in great fear of death,
from which I was miraculously preserved,
I, out of sheer gratitude to my Maker, did
incontinently make oath and sign articles to be one of the crew — which were
buccaneers. I did this the more readily
as we were to attack the ships of Spayne
only, and through there being no state
of Warre at that time between England
and that country, it was wisely conceived
that this conduct would provoke it, and
we should thus be forearmed, as became
a juste man in his quarrel. For this we
had the precious example of many great

Captains. We did therefore heave to and burn many ships — the quality of those engagements I do not set forth, not having a seaman's use of ship speech, and despising, as a plain, blunt man, those who misuse it, having it not.

But this I do know, that, having some conceit of a shipman's ways and of pirates, I did conceive at this time a pretty song for my comradoes, whereof the words ran thus : —

Yo ho ! when the Dog Watch bayeth loud
  In the light of a mid-sea moon!
And the Dead Eyes glare in the stiffening Shroud,
  For that is the Pirate's noon!
When the Night Mayres sit on the Dead Man's Chest
  Where no manne's breath may come —
Then hey for a bottle of Rum! Rum! Rum!
  And a passage to Kingdom come!

I take no credit to myself for the same, except so far as it may shew a touch of my Lord of Southampton's manner — we being intimate — but this I know, that it was much acclaimed by the crew. In-

deed they, observing that the Captain was
of a cruel nature, would fain kill him and
put me in his stead, but I, objecting to
the shedding of precious blood in such
behoof, did prevent such a lamentable and
inhuman action by stealthily throwing
him by night from his cabbin window into
the sea — where, owing to the inconceiv-
able distance of the ship from shore, he
was presently drowned. Which untoward
fate had a great effect upon my fortunes,
since, burthening myself with his goods
and effects, I found in his chest a printed
proclamation from an aged and infirm
clergyman in the West of England cove-
nanting that, for the sum of two crowns,
he would send to whoso offered, the chart
of an island of great treasure in the Spanish Main, whereof he had had confession
from the lips of a dying parishioner, and
the amount gained thereby he would use
for the restoration of his parish church.
Now I, reading this, was struck by a great

remorse and admiration for our late Captain, for that it would seem that he was,
like myself, a staunch upholder of the
Protestant Faith and the Church thereof,
as did appear by his possession of the
chart, for which he had no doubt paid the
two good crowns. As an act of penance
I resolved upon finding the same island
by the aid of the chart, and to that purpose sailed East many days, and South,
and North, and West as many other days
— the manner whereof and the latitude
and longitude of which I shall not burden
the reader with, holding it, as a plain,
blunt man, mere padding and imperti-
nence to fill out my narrative, which help-
eth not the general reader. So, I say,
when we sighted the Island, which seemed
to be swarming with savages, I ordered
the masts to be stripped, save but for a
single sail which hung sadly and distract-
edly, and otherwise put the ship into the
likeness of a forlorn wreck, clapping the

men, save one or two, under hatches. This I did to prevent the shedding of precious blood, knowing full well that the ignorant savages, believing the ship in sore distress, would swim off to her with provisions and fruit, bearing no arms. Which they did, while we, as fast as they clomb the sides, despatched them at leisure, without unseemly outcry or alarms. Having thus disposed of the most adventurous, we landed and took possession of the island, finding thereon many kegs of carbuncles and rubies and pieces of eight — the treasure store of those lawless pirates who infest the seas, having no colour of war or teaching of civilisation to atone for their horrid deeds.

I discovered also, by an omission in the chart, that this was not the Island wot of by the good and aged Devonshire divine — and so we eased our consciences of accounting for the treasure to him. We then sailed away, arriving after many years' absence at the Port of Bristol in Merrie England, where I took leave of the " Jolly Roger," that being the name of my ship; it was a strange conceit of seamen in after years ever to call the device of my *flag* — to wit, a skull and bones made in the sign of a Cross — by the *name* my ship bore, and if I have only corrected the misuse of history by lying knaves, I shall be content with this writing. But alas! such are the uncertainties of time; I found my good Lord of Southampton dead and most of his friends beheaded, and the blessed King James of Scotland — if I mistake not, for these also be the uncertainties of time — on the throne. In due time I married Mistress Marian Straitways. I might have told more of trifling, and how she fared, poor wench! in mine absence, even to the following of me in another ship, in a shipboy's disguise, and how I rescued her from a scheming Pagan villain; but, as a plain, blunt man, I am no hand at the weaving of puling love tales and such trifling diversions for love-sick mayds and their puny gallants — having only consideration for men and their deeds, which I have here set down bluntly and even at mine advanced years am ready to maintain with the hand that set it down.

DAN'L BOREM

By E. N-S W-T-T

DAN'L BOREM

I

DAN'L BOREM poured half of his second cup of tea abstractedly into his lap.

"Guess you've got suthin' on yer mind, Dan'l," said his sister.

"Mor'n likely I've got suthin' on my pants," returned Dan'l with that exquisitely dry, though somewhat protracted humor which at once thrilled and bored his acquaintances. "But — speakin' o' that hoss trade" —

"For goodness' sake, don't!" interrupted his sister wearily; "yer allus doin' it. Jest tell me about that young man — the new clerk ye think o' gettin'."

"Well, I telegraphed him to come over, arter I got this letter from him," he returned, handing her a letter.   "Read it out loud."

But his sister, having an experienced horror of prolixity, glanced over it.   "Far as I kin see he takes mor'n two hundred words to say you 've got to take him on trust, and sez it suthin' in a style betwixt a business circular and them Polite Letter Writers.   I thought you allowed he was a tony feller."

"Ef he does not brag much, ye see, I kin offer him small wages," said Dan'l, with a wink.   "It 's kinder takin' him at his own figger."

"And *that* might n't pay!   But ye don't think o' bringin' him *here* — in this house ?   'Cept you 're thinkin' o' tellin' him that yarn o' yours about the hoss trade to beguile the winter evenings.   I told ye ye 'd hev to pay yet to get folks to listen to it."

"Wrong agin — ez you 'll see !   Wot ef I get a hundred thousand folks to pay me for tellin' it? But, speakin' o' this young feller, I calkilated to send him to the Turkey Buzzard Hotel;" and he looked at his sister with a shrewd yet humorous smile.

"What!" said his sister in alarm. "The Turkey Buzzard! Why, he'll be starved or pizoned! He won't stay there a week."

"Ef he's pizoned to death he won't be able to demand any wages; ef he leaves because he can't stand it — it's proof positive he could n't stand me. Ef he's only starved and made weak and miserable he'll be easy to make terms with. It may seem hard what I'm sayin', but what seems hard on the other feller always comes mighty easy to you. The thing is *not* to be the 'other feller.' Ye ain't listenin'. Yet these remarks is shrewd and humorous, and hez bin thought so by literary fellers."

"H'm!" said his sister. "What's that ye was jest sayin' about folks bein' willin' to pay ye for tellin' that hoss trade yarn o' yours?"

"Thet's only what one o' them smart New York publishers allowed it was worth arter hearin' me tell it," said Dan'l dryly.

"Go way! You or him must be crazy. Why, it ain't ez good as that story 'bout a man who had a balky hoss that could be made to go only by buildin' a fire under him, and arter the man sells that hoss and the secret, and the man wot bought him tries it on, the blamed hoss lies down over the fire, and puts it out."

"I've allus allowed that the story ye hev to tell yourself is a blamed sight funnier than the one ye're listenin' to," said Dan'l. "Put that down among my sayin's, will ye?"

"But your story was never anythin' more than one o' them snippy things ye see in the papers, drored out to no end by you. It's only one o' them funny paragraphs ye kin read in a minit in the papers that takes *you* an hour to tell."

To her surprise Dan'l only looked at his sister with complacency.

"That," he said, "is jest what the New York publisher sez. 'The 'Merrikan people,' sez he, 'is ashamed o' bein' short and peart and funny; it lacks dignity,' sez he; 'it looks funny,' sez he, 'but it ain't deep-seated nash'nul literature,' sez he. 'Them snips o' funny stories and short dialogues in the comic papers — they make ye laff,' sez he, 'but laffin' is n't no sign o' deep morril purpose,' sez he, 'and it ain't genteel and refined. Abraham Linkin with his pat anecdotes ruined our standin' with dignified nashuns,' sez he. 'We cultivated publishers is sick o' hearin' furrin' nashuns roarin' over funny 'Merrikan stories; we 're goin' to show 'em that, even ef we have n't classes and titles and sich, we kin be dull. We 're workin' the historical racket for

all that it's worth, — ef we can't **go**
back mor'n a hundred years or so, we kin
rake in a Lord and a Lady when we do,
and we're gettin' in some ole-fashioned
spellin' and "methinkses" and "perad-
ventures." We're doin' the religious bizness ez slick ez Robert Elsmere, and we
find lots o' soul in folks — and heaps o'
quaint morril characters,' sez he."

"Sakes alive, Dan'l!" broke in his
sister; "what's all that got to do with
your yarn 'bout the hoss trade?"

"Everythin'," returned Dan'l. "'For,'
sez he, 'Mr. Borem,' sez he, 'you're
a quaint morril character. You've got
protracted humor,' sez he. 'You've bin
an hour tellin' that yarn o' yours! Ef
ye could spin it out to fill two chapters
of a book — yer fortune's made! For
you'll show that a successful hoss trade
involves the highest nash'nul character-
istics. That what common folk calls
"selfishness," "revenge," "mean lyin',"

and " low - down money - grubbin' ambishun " is really " quaintness," and will go in double harness with the bizness of a Christian banker,' sez he."

" Created goodness, Dan'l! You 're designin' ter " —

Dan'l Borem rose, coughed, expectorated carefully at the usual spot in the fender, his general custom of indicating the conclusion of a subject or an interview, and said dryly : " I 'm thar ! "

II

To return to the writer of the letter, whose career was momentarily cut off by the episode of the horse trade (who, if he had previously received a letter written by somebody else would have been an entirely different person and not in this novel at all) : John Lummox — known to his family as "the perfect Lummox" — had been two years in college, but thought it rather fine of himself — a habit of thought in which he frequently indulged — to become a clerk, but finally got tired of it, and to his father's relief went to Europe for a couple of years, returning with some knowledge of French and German, and the cutting end of a German student's blunted dueling sword. Having, as he felt, thus equipped himself for the hero

of an American " Good Society " novel,
he went on board a " liner," where there
would naturally be susceptible young
ladies. One he thought he recognized
as a girl with whom he used to play
" forfeits " in the vulgar past of his boyhood. She sat at his table, accompanied
by another lady whose husband seemed to
be a confirmed dyspeptic. His remarks
struck Lummox as peculiar.

" Shall I begin dinner with pudding
and cheese or take the ordinary soup first ?
I quite forget which I did last night," he
said anxiously to his wife.

But Mrs. Starling hesitated.

" Tell me, Mary," he said, appealing to
Miss Bike, the young lady.

" I should begin with the pudding,"
said Miss Bike decisively, " and between
that and the arrival of the cheese you can
make up your mind, and then, if you think
better, go back to the soup."

" Thank you so much. Now, as to

drink ? Shall I take the Friedrichshalle first or the Benedictine ? You know the doctor insists upon the Friedrichshalle, but I don't think I did well to mix them as I did yesterday. Or shall I take simply milk and beer ? "

" I should say simplicity was best. Besides, you can always fill up with champagne later."

How splendidly this clear-headed, clear-eyed girl dominated the man ! Lummox felt that *really* he might renew her acquaintance ! He did so.

" I remembered you," she said. " You 've not changed a bit since you were eight years old."

John, wishing to change the subject, said that he thought Mr. Starling seemed an uncertain man.

" Very ! He 's even now in his state-room sitting in his pyjamas with a rubber shoe on one foot and a pump on the other, wondering whether he ought to put on

golf knickerbockers with a dressing-gown
and straw hat before he comes on deck.
He has already put on and taken off about
twenty suits."

" He certainly is very trying," returned
Lummox. He paused and colored deeply.
"I beg," he stammered, "I hope — you
don't think me guilty of a pun ! When
I said 'trying' I referred entirely to the
effect on your sensitiveness of these ten-
tative attempts toward clothing himself."

"I should never accuse *you* of levity,
Mr. Lummox," said the young lady, gazing thoughtfully upon his calm but somewhat heavy features, — " never."

Yet he would have liked to reclaim himself by a show of lightness. He was leaning on the rail looking at the sea. The
scene was beautiful.

" I suppose," he said, rolling with the
sea and his early studies of Doctor Johnson, " that one would in the more superior manner show his appreciation of all

this by refraining from the obvious com-
ment which must needs be recognized as
comparatively commonplace and vulgar;
but really this is so superb that I must
express some of my emotion, even at the
risk of lowering your opinion of my good
taste, provided, of course, that you have
any opinion on the one hand or any good
taste on the other."

"Without that undue depreciation of
one's self which must ever be a sign of
self-conscious demerit," said the young
girl lightly, "I may say that I am not
generally good at Johnsonese; but it may
relieve your mind to know that had you
kept silence one instant longer, I should
have taken the risk of lowering your opinion of my taste, provided, of course, that
you have one to lower and are capable of
that exertion —if such indeed it may be
termed — by remarking that this is perfectly magnificent."

"Do you think," he said gloomily, still

leaning on the rail, "that we can keep
this kind of thing up — perhaps I should
say down — much longer? For myself,
I am feeling far from well; it may have
been the lobster — or that last sentence
— but " —

They were both silent. "Yet," she
said, after a pause, "you can at least take
Mr. Starling and his dyspepsia off my
hands. You might be equal to that exertion."

"I suppose that by this time I ought
to be doing something for somebody,"
he said thoughtfully. "Yes, I will."

That evening after dinner he took Mr.
Starling into the smoking-room and card-
room. They had something hot. At 4
A. M., with the assistance of the steward,
he projected Mr. Starling into Mrs. Starling's stateroom, delicately withdrawing
to evade the lady's thanks. At breakfast he saw Miss Bike. "Thank you so
much," she said; "Mrs. Starling found

Starling greatly improved. He himself
admitted he was 'never berrer' and, far
from worrying about what night-clothes
he should wear, went to bed *as he was* —
even to his hat. Mrs. Starling calls you
'her preserver,' and Mr. Starling distinctly
stated that you were a 'jolly-good-fler.'"

"And you?" asked John Lummox.

"In your present condition of abnormal
self-consciousness and apperceptive ego-
tism, I really should n't like to say."

When the voyage was ended Mr. Lummox went to see Mary Bike at her house,
and his father — whom he had not seen
for ten years — at *his* house. With a
refined absence of natural affection he
contented himself with inquiring of the
servants as to his father's habits, and if
he still wore dress clothes at dinner. The
information thus elicited forced him to
the conclusion that the old gentleman's
circumstances were reduced, and that it
was possible that he, John Lummox, might

be actually compelled to earn his own
living. He communicated that suspicion
to his father at dinner, and over the
last bottle of " Mouton," a circumstance
which also had determined him in his
resolution. " You might," said his father
thoughtfully, " offer yourself to some rising American novelist as a study for the
new hero, — one absolutely without ambition, capacity, or energy; willing, however, to be whatever the novelist chooses
to make him, so long as he has n't to
choose for himself. If your inordinate
self-consciousness is still in your way, I
could give him a few points about you,
myself."

"I had thought," said John, hesitatingly, " of going into your office and becoming your partner in the business. You
could always look after me, you know."

A shudder passed over the old man.
Then he tremblingly muttered to himself:
" Thank heaven! There is one way it

may still be averted!" Retiring to his room he calmly committed suicide, thoughtfully leaving the empty poison bottle in the fender.

And this is how John Lummox came to offer himself as a clerk to Dan'l Borem. The ways of Providence are indeed strange, yet those of the novelist are only occasionally novel.

III

JOHN K. LUMMOX lived for a week at the Turkey Buzzard Hotel exclusively on doughnuts and innuendoes. He was informed by Mr. Borem's clerk — whose place he was to fill — that he would n't be able to stand it, and thus received the character of his employer from his last employee.

" I suppose," said Dan'l Borem, chuckling, " that he said I was a old skinflint, good only at a hoss trade, uneddicated, ignorant, and unable to keep accounts, and an oppressor o' the widder and orphan. Allowed that my cute sayin's was a kind o' ten-cent parody o' them proverbs in Poor Richard's Almanack ! "

" Omitting a few expletives, he certainly did," returned Lummox with great delicacy.

" He allowed to me," said Dan'l thought-fully, " that *you* was a poor critter that had n't a single reason to show for livin' : that the fool-killer had bin shadderin' you from your birth, and that you had n't paid a cent profit on your father's original investment in ye, nor on the assessments he 'd paid on ye ever since. He seems to be a cute feller arter all, and I 'm rather sorry he 's leavin'."

" I am quite willing to abandon my posi-tion in his favor, now," said Lummox with alacrity.

" No," said Dan'l, rubbing his chin argumentatively ; "the only way for us to do is to circumvent him like in a hoss trade — with suthin' unexpected. When he thinks you 're goin' to sleep in the shafts you 'll run away ; and when he thinks I 'm vicious I 'll let a woman or a child drive me."

IV

"WELL, Dan'l, how's that new clerk o' yours gettin' on?" said Mrs. Bigby a week later.

"Purty fine! He's good at accounts and hez got to know the Bank's customers by this time. But I allus reckoned he'd get stuck with some o' them counterfeit notes — and he hez! Ye see he ain't accustomed to look at a five or a ten dollar note as sharp as some men, and he's already taken in two tens and a five counterfeits."

"Gracious!" said Mrs. Bigsby. "What did the poor feller do?"

"Oh, he ups and tells me, all right, after he discovered it. And sez he: 'I've charged my account with 'em,' sez he, 'so the Bank won't lose it.'"

"Why, Dan'l," said Mrs. Bigsby, "ye did n't let that poor feller" —

"You hol' on!" said her brother; "business is business; but I sez to him: 'Ye oughter put it down to Profit and Loss account. Or perhaps we'll have a chance o' gettin' rid o' them, — not in Noo York, where folks is sharp, but here in the country, and then ye kin credit yourself with the amount arter you've got rid o' them.'"

"Laws! I 'm sorry ye did that, Dan'l," said Mrs. Bigsby.

"With that he riz up," continued Dan'l, ignoring his sister, "and, takin' them counterfeit notes from my hand, sez he: 'Them notes belong to *me* now,' sez he, 'and I 'm goin' to destroy 'em.' And with that he walks over to the fire as stiff as a poker, and held them notes in it until they were burnt clean up."

"Well, but that was honest and straightforward in him!" said Mrs. Bigsby.

"Um! but it was n't business — and ye see " — Dan'l paused and rubbed his chin.

"Well, go on!" said Mrs. Bigsby impatiently.

"Well, ye see, neither him nor me was very smart in detectin' counterfeits, or even knowin' 'em, and "—

"Well! For goodness' sake, Dan'l, speak out!"

"Well — *the dum fool burnt up three good bills,* and we neither of us knew it!"

V

THE "unexpected" which Dan'l Borem had hinted might characterize his future conduct was first intimated by his treatment of the "Widow Cully," an aged and impoverished woman whose property was heavily mortaged to him. He had curtly summoned her to come to his office on Christmas Day and settle up. Frightened, hopeless, and in the face of a snowstorm, the old woman attended, but was surprised by receiving a "satisfaction piece" in full from the banker, and a gorgeous Christmas dinner. "All the same," said Mrs. Bigsby to Lummox, "Dan'l might hev done all this without frightenin' the poor old critter into a nervous fever, chillin' her through by makin' her walk two miles through the

snow, and keepin' her on the ragged
edge o' despair for two mortal hours!
But it's his humorous way."

"Did he give any reason for being so
lenient to the widow?" asked Lummox.

"He said that her son had given him
a core of his apple when they were boys
together.   Dan'l ez mighty thoughtful
o' folks that was kind to him in them
days."

"Is that all?" said Lummox, astonished.

"Well — I've kinder thought suthin'
else," said Mrs. Bigsby hesitatingly.

"What?"

"That its bein' Christmas Day — and
as I've heard tell that's *no day in law*,
but just like Sunday — Dan'l mebbe
thought that he might crawl outer that
satisfaction piece, ef he ever wanted ter!
Dan'l is mighty cute."

Mr. John Lummox was not behind his employer in developing unexpected traits of character. Hitherto holding aloof from his neighbors in Old Folksville, he suddenly went to a social gathering, and distinguished himself as the principal and popular guest of the evening. As Dan'l Borem afterward told his sister: " He was one o' them Combination Minstrels and Variety Shows in one. He sang through a whole opery, made the pianner jest howl, gave some recitations, Casabianker and Betsy and I are Out; imitated all them tragedians; did tricks with cards and fetched rabbits outer hats, besides liftin' the pianner with two men sittin' on it, jest by his teeth. Created snakes ! " said Borem, concluding his account, which here is necessarily abbreviated, " ef he learnt all that in his two years in Europe I ain't sayin' anythin' more agin' eddication and furrin' travel after this! Why, the next day there was quite a run on the Bank jest to see *him*. He is makin' the bizness pop'lar."

" Then ye think ye 'll get along together ? "

" I reckon we 'll hitch hosses," said Dan'l, with a smile.

A few weeks later, one evening, Dan'l Borem sat with his sister alone. John Lummox, who was now residing with them, was attending a social engagement. Mrs. Bigsby knew that Dan'l had something to communicate, but knew that he would do so in his own way.

" Speakin' o' hoss trades," he began.

" We *was n't* and we ain't goin' to," said Mrs. Bigsby with great promptness. " I 've heard enough of 'em."

" But this here one hez suthin' to do

with your fr'en', John Lummox," said
Dan'l, with a chuckle.

Mrs. Bigsby stared. "Go on, then,"
she said, "but, for goodness' sake, cut it
short."

Dan'l threw away his quid and replenished it from his silver tobacco box. Mrs.
Bigsby shuddered slightly as she recognized the usual preliminary to prolixity,
but determined, as far as possible, to make
her brother brief.

"It mout be two weeks ago," began
Dan'l, "that I see John Lummox over at
Palmyra, where he'd bin visitin'. He
was drivin' a hoss, the beautifulest critter — for color — I ever saw. It was
yaller, with mane and tail a kinder golden,
like the hair o' them British Blondes that
was here in the Variety Show."

"Dan'l!" exclaimed Mrs. Bigsby, horrified. "And you allowed you never went
thar!"

"Saw 'em on the posters — and mebbe

the color was a little brighter thar," said Dan'l carelessly — " but who 's interruptin' now ? "

" Go on," said Mrs. Bigsby.

" ' Got a fine hoss thar,' sez I ; ' reckon I never see such a purty color,' sez I. ' He is purty,' sez he, ' per'aps too purty for *me* to be a-drivin', but he is n't fast.' ' I ain't speakin' o' that,' sez I ; ' it 's his looks that I 'm talkin' of ; whar might ye hev got him ? ' ' He was offered to me by a fr'en' o' me boyhood,' sez he ; ' he 's a *pinto* mustang,' sez he, ' from Californy, whar they breed 'em.' ' What 's a *pinto* hoss ? ' sez I. ' The same ez a calico hoss,' sez he ; ' what they have in cirkises, but ye never see 'em that color.' En he was right, for when I looked him over I never *did* see such a soft and silky coat, and his mane and tail jest glistened. ' It *is* a little too showy for ye,' sez I, ' but *I* might take him at a fair price. What 's your fr'en' askin' ? ' ' He won't sell him to anybody but me,' sez Lummox; 'he's a horror o' hoss traders, anyway, and his price is more like a gift to a fr'en'.' ' What might that price be, ef it's a fair question?' sez I, for the more I looked at the hoss the more I liked him. 'A hundred and fifty dollars,' sez he; 'but my fr'en' would ask *you* double that.' ' Could n't *you* and *me* make a trade?' sez I; 'I'll exchange ye that roan mare, that's worth two hundred, for this hoss and fifty dollars.' With that he drew himself up, and sez he: 'Mr. Borem,' sez he, ' I share my fr'en's opinion about hoss tradin', and I promised my mother I'd never swap hosses. You ought to know me by this time.' "

" That's so ! " said Mrs. Bigsby; " I'm wonderin' ye dared to ax him."

Dan'l passed his hand over his mouth, and continued: " 'I dunno but you're right, Lummox,' sez I; ' per'aps it's jest as well as thar was n't *two* in the Bank in that bizness.' But the more I looked at the hoss the more I hankered arter him. 'Look here,' sez I, 'I tell ye what I'll do! I'll *lend* you my hoss and you'll *lend* me yourn. I'll draw up a paper to that effect, and provide that in case o' accidents, ef I don't return you your hoss, I'll agree to pay you a hundred and fifty dollars. You'll give me the same kind o' paper about my hoss — with the proviso that you pay me two hundred for him!' 'Excuse me, Mr. Borem,' sez he, ' but that difference of fifty makes a hoss trade accordin' to my mind. It's agin' my principles to make such an agreement.' "

" An' he was right, Dan'l," said Mrs. Bigsby approvingly.

But Dan'l wiped his mouth again, leaving, however, a singular smile on it. " Well, ez I wanted that hoss, I jest thought and thought! I knew I could get two hundred and fifty for him easy,

and that Lummox did n't know anythin'
of his valoo, and I finally agreed to make
the swap even. 'What do you call him?'
sez I. 'Pegasus,' sez he, — 'the poet's
hoss, on account o' his golden mane,' sez
he. That made me laff, for I never knew
a poet ez could afford to hev a hoss, —
much less one like that! But I said:
'I'll borry Pegasus o' you on those terms.'
The next day I took the hoss to Jonesville;
Lummox was right: he was n't *fast*, but,
jest as I expected, he made a sensation!
Folks crowded round him whenever I
stopped; wimmin followed him and children cried for him. I could hev sold
him for three hundred without leavin'
town! 'So ye call him Pegasus,' sez
Doc Smith, grinnin'; 'I did n't known
ye was subject to the divine afflatus, Dan'l.'
'I don' offen hev it,' sez I, 'but when
I do I find a little straight gin does me
good.' 'So did Byron,' sez he, chucklin'.
But even if I had called him 'Beelze-

bub' the hull town would hev bin jest as crazy over him. Well, as it was comin' on to rain I started jest after sundown for home. But it came ter blow, an' ter pour cats and dogs, an' I was nigh washed out o' the buggy, besides losin' my way and gettin' inter ditches and puddles, and I hed to stop at Staples' Half-Way House and put up for the night. In the mornin' I riz up early and goes into the stable yard, and the first thing I sees was the 'ostler. 'I hope ye giv' my hoss a good scrub down,' I sez, 'as I told ye, for his color is that delicate the smallest spot shows. It's a very rare color for a hoss.' 'I was hopin' it might be,' sez he. I was a little huffed at that, and I sez: 'It's considered a very beautiful color.' 'Mebbe it is,' sez he, 'but I never cared much for fireworks.' 'What yer mean?' sez I. 'Look here, Squire!' sez he; 'I don't mind scourin' and rubbin' down a hoss that will stay the same color *twice*,

but when he gets to playin' a kaladeo-
skope on me, I kick!' 'Trot him out,'
sez I, beginnin' to feel queer. With that
he fetched out the hoss! For a minit I
hed to ketch on to the fence to keep myself from fallin'. I swonny! ef he did n't
look like a case of measles on top o' yaller fever — 'cept where the harness had
touched him, and that was kinder sten-
ciled out all over him. Thar was places
whar the 'ostler had washed down to the
foundation color, a kind o' chewed lico-
rice! Then I knew that somebody had bin
sold terrible, and I reckoned it might be
me! But I said nothin' to the 'ostler, and
waited until dark, when I drove him over
here, and put him in the stables, lettin'
no one see him. In the mornin' Lummox
comes to me, and sez he: 'I'm glad to
see you back,' sez he, 'for my conscience
is troublin' me about that hoss agreement;
it looks too much like a hoss trade,' sez he,
'and I'm goin' to send the hoss back.'

'Mebbe your conscience,' sez I, 'may trouble you a little more ef you'll step this way;' and with that I takes his arm and leads him round to the stable and brings out the hoss.

"Well, Lummox never changes ez much as a hair, ez he puts up his eye-glasses. 'I'm not good at what's called "Pop'lar Art,"' sez he. 'Is it a chromo, or your own work?' sez he, critical like.

"'It's *your hoss*,' sez I.

"He looks at me a minit and then drors a paper from his pocket. 'This paper,' sez he in his quiet way, 'was drored up by you and is a covenant to return to me a yaller hoss with golden mane and tail — or a hundred and fifty dollars. Ez I don't see the hoss anywhere — mebbe you've got the hundred and fifty dollars handy?' sez he. 'Suppose I had n't the money?' sez I. 'I should be obliged,' sez he in a kind o' pained Christian-martyr way, 'ter sell *your* hoss for two hundred, and send the money to my fr'en'.' We looked at each other steddy for a minit and then I counts him out a hundred and fifty. He took the money sad-like and then sez: 'Mr. Borem,' sez he, 'this is a great morril lesson to us,' and went back to the office. In the arternoon I called in an old hoss dealer that I knew and shows him Pegasus.

"'He wants renewin',' sez he.

"'Wot's that?' sez I.

"'A few more bottles o' that British Blonde Hair Dye to set him up ag'in. That's wot they allus do in the cirkis, whar he kem from.'

"Then I went back to the office and I took down my sign. 'What's that you're doin'?' sez Lummox, with a sickly kind o' smile. 'Are you goin' out o' the bizness?'

"'No, I'm only goin' to change that sign from "Dan'l Borem" to "Borem and Lummox,"' sez I. 'I've concluded

it 's cheaper for me to take you inter part-
nership now than to continue in this way,
which would only end in your hevin' to
take me in later. I preferred to *do it
fust.*' "

A RICH man, and settled in business, John Lummox concluded that he would marry Mary Bike. With that far-sighted logic which had always characterized him he reasoned that, having first met her on a liner, he would find her again on one if he took passage to Europe. He did — but she was down on the passenger list as Mrs. Edwin Wraggles. The result of their interview was given to Mrs. Bigsby by Dan'l Borem in his own dialect.

"Ez far as I kin see, it was like the Deacon's Sunday hoss trade, bein' all 'Ef it wassent.' 'Ef ye was n't Mrs. Wraggles,' sez Lummox, sez he, 'I'd be tellin' ye how I've loved ye ever sence I first seed ye. Ef ye was n't Mrs. Wraggles, I'd be squeezin' yer hand,' sez he; 'ef

ye was n't Mrs. Wraggles, I 'd be askin'
ye to marry me.' Then the gal ups and
sez, sez she : ' But I *ain't* Mrs. Wraggles,'
sez she ; ' Mrs. Wraggles is my sister, and
could n't come, so I 'm travelin' on her
ticket, and that 's how my name is Wraggles on the passenger list.' ' But why
did n't ye tell me so at once ? ' sez Lummox. ' This is an episoode o' protracted
humor,' sez she, ' and *I 'm* bound to have
a show in it somehow ! ' "

"Well ! " said Mrs. Bigsby breathlessly ;
"then he *did* marry her ? "

"Darned ef I know. He never said
so straight out — but that 's like Lummox."

STORIES THREE

By R–DY–D K–PL–G

I

FOR SIMLA REASONS

Some people say that improbable things don't necessarily happen in India — but these people never find improbabilities anywhere. This sounds clever, but you will at once perceive that it really means the opposite of what I intended to say. So we'll drop it. What I am trying to tell you is that after Sparkley had that affair with Miss Millikens a singular change came over him. He grew abstracted and solitary, — holding dark séances with himself, — which was odd, as everybody knew he never cared a rap for the Millikens girl. It was even said that he was off his head — which is rhyme. But his reason was undoubtedly affected, for he had been heard to mutter incoherently at the Club, and, strangest of all, to answer questions *that were never asked!* This was so awkward in that Branch of the Civil Department of which he was a high official — where the rule was exactly the reverse — that he was presently invalided on full pay! Then he disappeared. Clever people said it was because the Department was afraid he had still much to answer for; stupid people simply envied him.

Mrs. Awksby, whom everybody knew had been the cause of breaking off the match, was now wild to know the reason of Sparkley's retirement. She attacked heaven and earth, and even went a step higher — to the Viceroy. At the vice-regal ball I saw, behind the curtains of a window, her rolling violet-blue eyes with a singular glitter in them. It was the reflection of the Viceroy's star, although the rest of his Excellency was hidden in the curtain. I heard him say-

ing, " Come now! really, now, you are
— you know you are!" in reply to her
cooing questioning.   Then she made a
dash at me and captured me.

" What did you hear?"

" Nothing I should not have heard."

" Don't be like all the other men —
you silly boy!" she answered.   "I was
only trying to find out something about
Sparkley.   And I will find it out, too,"
she said, clinching her thin little hand.
" And what's more," she added, turning
on me suddenly, " *you* shall help me!"

" I?" I said in surprise.

" Don't pretend!" she said poutingly.
" You're too clever to believe he's cut
up over the Millikens.   No — it's something awful or — another woman!   Now,
if I knew as much of India as you do
— and was n't a woman, and could go
where I liked — I 'd go to Bungloore and
find him."

" Oh!   You have his address?" I said.

"Certainly! What did you expect I
was behind the curtain with the Viceroy
for?" she said, opening her violet eyes
innocently. "It's Bunglooré — First
Turning to the Right — At the End of
the Passage."

Bunglooré — near Ghouli Pass — in
the Jungle! I knew the place, a spot
of dank pestilence and mystery. "You
never could have gone there," I said.

"You do not know *what* I could do
for a *friend*," she said sweetly, veiling
her eyes in demure significance.

"Oh, come off the roof!" I said bluntly.

She could be obedient when it was
necessary. She came off. Not without
her revenge. "Try to remember you are
not at school with the Stalkies," she said,
and turned away.

I went to Bunglooré, — not on her
account, but my own. If you don't know
India, you won't know Bunglooré. It's
all that and more. An egg dropped by

a vulture, sat upon and addled by the Department. But I knew the house and
walked boldly in. A lion walked out of
one door as I came in at another. We
did this two or three times — and found
it amusing. A large cobra in the hall
rose up, bowed as I passed, and respectfully removed his hood.

I found the poor old boy at the end of
the passage. It might have been the
passage between Calais and Dover, — he
looked so green, so limp and dejected. I
affected not to notice it, and threw myself
in a chair.

He gazed at me for a moment and then
said, " Did you hear what the chair was
saying ? "

It was an ordinary bamboo armchair,
and had creaked after the usual fashion
of bamboo chairs. I said so.

He cast his eyes to the ceiling. " He
calls it ' creaking,' " he murmured. " No
matter," he continued aloud, " its remark

was not of a complimentary nature. It's very difficult to get really polite furniture."

The man was evidently stark, staring mad. I still affected not to observe it, and asked him if that was why he left Simla.

"There were Simla reasons, certainly," he replied. "But you think I came here for solitude! *Solitude!*" he repeated, with a laugh. "Why, I hold daily conversations with any blessed thing in this house, from the veranda to the chimney-stack, with any stick of furniture, from the footstool to the towel-horse. I get more out of it than the gabble at the Club. You look surprised. Listen! I took this thing up in my leisure hours in the Department. I had read much about the conversation of animals. I argued that if animals conversed, why shouldn't in-animate things communicate with each other? You cannot prove that animals don't converse — neither can you prove that inanimate objects *do not.* See ? "

I was thunderstruck with the force of his logic.

" Of course," he continued, " there are degrees of intelligence, and that makes it difficult. For instance, a mahogany table would not talk like a rush-bottomed kitchen chair." He stopped suddenly, listened, and replied, " I really could n't say."

"I did n't speak," I said.

" I know *you* did n't. But your chair asked me ' how long that fool was going to stay.' I replied as you heard. Pray don't move — I intend to change that chair for one more accustomed to polite society. To continue : I perfected myself in the language, and it was awfully jolly at first. Whenever I went by train, I heard not only all the engines said, but what every blessed carriage thought, that joined in the conversation. If you chaps only knew what rot those whistles can get

13—v. 5

off! And as for the brakes, they can beat
any mule driver in cursing. Then, after
a time, it got rather monotonous, and I
took a short sea trip for my health. But,
by Jove, every blessed inch of the whole
ship — from the screw to the bowsprit —
had something to say, and the bad language used by the garboard strake when
the ship rolled was something too awful!
You don't happen to know what the garboard strake is, do you?"

"No," I replied.

"No more do I. That's the dreadful
thing about it. You've got to listen to
chaps that you don't know. Why, coming home on my bicycle the other day
there was an awful row between some infernal 'sprocket' and the 'ball bearings'
of the machine, and I never knew before
there were such things in the whole concern."

I thought I had got at his secret, and
said carelessly: "Then I suppose this was

the reason why you broke off your engagement with Miss Millikens ? "

" Not at all," he said coolly. " Nothing to do with it. That is quite another affair. It's a very queer story ; would you like to hear it ? "

" By all means." I took out my notebook.

" You remember that night of the Amateur Theatricals, got up by the White Hussars, when the lights suddenly went out all over the house ? "

"Yes," I replied, " I heard about it."

" Well, I had gone down there that evening with the determination of proposing to Mary Millikens the first chance that offered. She sat just in front of me, her sister Jane next, and her mother, smart Widow Millikens, — who was a bit larky on her own account, you remember, — the next on the bench. When the lights went out and the panic and tittering began, I saw my chance ! I leaned forward, and in a voice that would just reach Mary's ear I said, ' I have long wished to tell you how my life is bound up with you, dear, and I never, never can be happy without you ' — when just then there was a mighty big shove down my bench from the fellows beyond me, who were trying to get out. But I held on like grim death, and struggled back again into position, and went on : ' You 'll forgive my taking a chance like this, but I felt I could no longer conceal my love for you,' when I 'm blest if there was n't another shove, and though I 'd got hold of her little hand and had a kind of squeeze in return, I was drifted away again and had to fight my way back. But I managed to finish, and said, ' If the devotion of a lifetime will atone for this hurried avowal of my love for you, let me hope for a response,' and just then the infernal lights were turned on, and there I was holding the widow's hand and she nestling on my shoulder, and the

two girls in hysterics on the other side.
You see, I never knew that they were
shoved down on their bench every time,
just as I was, and of course when I got
back to where I was I'd just skipped one
of them each time! Yes, sir! I had
made that proposal in *three* sections — a
part to each girl, winding up with the
mother! No explanation was possible,
and I left Simla next day. Naturally, it
was n't a thing they could talk about,
either!"

"Then you think Mrs. Awksby had
nothing to do with it?" I said.

"Nothing — absolutely nothing. By
the way, if you see that lady, you might
tell her that I have possession of that
brocade easy-chair which used to stand in
the corner of her boudoir. You remember it, — faded white and yellow, with one
of the casters off and a little frayed at the
back, but rather soft-spoken and amiable?
But of course you don't understand *that*.

I bought it after she moved into her new bungalow."

"But why should I tell her that?" I asked in wonder.

" Nothing — except that I find it very amusing with its reminiscences of the company she used to entertain, and her confidences generally. Good-by — take care of the lion in the hall. He always couches on the left for a spring. Ta-ta ! "

I hurried away. When I returned to Simla I told Mrs. Awksby of my discoveries, and spoke of the armchair.

I fancied she colored slightly, but quickly recovered.

" Dear old Sparkley," she said sweetly ; " he *was* a champion liar ! "

II

A PRIVATE'S HONOR

I HAD not seen Mulledwiney for several days. Knowing the man — this looked bad. So I dropped in on the Colonel. I found him in deep thought. This looked bad, too, for old Cockey Wax — as he was known to everybody in the Hill districts but himself — was n't given to thinking. I guessed the cause and told him so.

" Yes," he said wearily, " you are right! It 's the old story. Mulledwiney, Bleareyed, and Otherwise are at it again, — drink followed by Clink. Even now two corporals and a private are sitting on Mulledwiney's head to keep him quiet, and Bleareyed is chained to an elephant."

" Perhaps," I suggested, " you are unnecessarily severe."

" Do you really think so? Thank you *so* much! I am always glad to have a civilian's opinion on military matters — and *vice versa* — it broadens one so! And yet — am I severe? I am willing, for instance, to overlook their raid upon a native village, and the ransom they demanded for a native inspector! I have overlooked their taking the horses out of my carriage for their own use. I am content also to believe that my fowls meekly succumb to jungle fever and cholera. But there are some things I cannot ignore. The carrying off of the great god Vishnu from the Sacred Shrine at Ducidbad by The Three for the sake of the priceless opals in its eyes " —

" But I never heard of *that*," I interrupted eagerly. " Tell me."

" Ah!" said the Colonel playfully, " that — as you so often and so amusingly say — is ' Another Story '! Yet I would have overlooked the theft of the opals if they had not substituted two of the Queen's regimental buttons for the eyes of the god. This, while it did not deceive the ignorant priests, had a deep political and racial significance. You are aware, of course, that the great mutiny was occasioned by the issue of cartridges to the native troops greased with hog's fat — forbidden by their religion."

"But these three men could themselves alone quell a mutiny," I replied.

The Colonel grasped my hand warmly. "Thank you. So they could. I never thought of that." He looked relieved. For all that, he presently passed his hand over his forehead and nervously chewed his cheroot.

"There is something else," I said.

"You are right. There is. It is a secret. Promise me it shall go no further — than the Press? Nay, swear that you will *keep* it for the Press!"

"I promise."

"Thank you *so* much.   It is a matter
of my own and Mulledwiney's.   The fact
is, we have had a *personal* difficulty."
He paused, glanced around him, and continued in a low, agitated voice : "Yesterday I came upon him as he was sitting
leaning against the barrack wall.   In a
spirit of playfulness — mere playfulness,
I assure you, sir — I poked him lightly
in the shoulder with my stick, saying
'Boo!'   He turned — and I shall never
forget the look he gave me."

"Good heavens!" I gasped, "you
touched — absolutely *touched* — Mulledwiney?"

"Yes," he said hurriedly, "I knew
what you would say ; it was against the
Queen's Regulations — and — there was
his sensitive nature which shrinks from
even a harsh word ; but I did it, and of
course he has me in his power."

"And you have touched him?" I repeated, — "touched his private honor!"

" Yes ! But I shall atone for it ! I have already arranged with him that we shall have it out between ourselves alone, in the jungle, stripped to the buff, with our fists — Queensberry rules ! I have n't fought since I stood up against Spinks Major — you remember old Spinks, now of the Bombay Offensibles ? — at Eton." And the old boy pluckily bared his skinny arm.

" It may be serious," I said.

" I have thought of that. I have a wife, several children, and an aged parent in England. If I fall, they must never know. You must invent a story for them. I have thought of cholera, but that is played out; you know we have already tried it on The Boy who was Thrown Away. Invent something quiet, peaceable and respectable — as far removed from fighting as possible. What do you say to measles ? "

" Not half bad," I returned.

"Measles let it be, then! Say I caught it from Wee Willie Winkie. You do not think it too incredible?" he added timidly.

"Not more than *your* story," I said.

He grasped my hand, struggling violently with his emotion. Then he struggled with me — and I left hurriedly. Poor old boy! The funeral was well attended, however, and no one knew the truth, not even myself.

III

JUNGLE FOLK

It was high noon of a warm summer's day when Moo Kow came down to the watering-place. Miaow, otherwise known as "Puskat" — the warmth-loving one — was crouching on a limb that overhung the pool, sunning herself. Brer Rabbit — but that is Another Story by Another Person.

Three or four Gee Gees, already at the pool, moved away on the approach of Moo Kow.

"Why do ye stand aside?" said the Moo Kow.

"Why do you say 'ye'?" said the Gee Gees together.

"Because it's more impressive than 'you.' Don't you know that all animals talk that way in English?" said the Moo Kow.

"And they also say 'thou,' and don't you forget it!" interrupted Miaow from the tree. "I learnt that from a Man Cub."

The animals were silent. They did not like Miaow's slang, and were jealous of her occasionally sitting on a Man Cub's lap. Once Dun-kee, a poor relation of the Gee Gees, had tried it on, disastrously — but that is also Another and a more Aged Story.

"We are ridden by The English — please to observe the Capital letters," said Pi Böl, the leader of the Gee Gees, proudly. "They are a mighty race who ride anything and everybody. D' ye mind that — I mean, look ye well to it!"

"What should they know of England who only England know?" said Miaow.

"Is that a conundrum?" asked the Moo Kow.

"No; it 's poetry," said the Miaow.

"I know England," said Pi Böl pran-

cingly. " I used to go from the Bank to
Islington three times a day — I mean,"
he added hurriedly, " before I became a
screw — I should say, a screw-gun horse."

" And I," said the Moo Kow, " am terrible. When the young women and children in the village see me approach they
fly shriekingly. My presence alone has
scattered their sacred festival — The
Sundés Kool Piknik. I strike terror to
their inmost souls, and am more feared by
them than even Kreep-mows, the insidi-
ous! And yet, behold! I have taken
the place of the mothers of men, and I
have nourished the mighty ones of the
earth! But that," said the Moo Kow,
turning her head aside bashfully, " that
is Anudder Story."

A dead silence fell on the pool.

" And I," said Miaow, lifting up her
voice, " I am the horror and haunter of
the night season. When I pass like the
night wind over the roofs of the houses

men shudder in their beds and tremble. When they hear my voice as I creep stealthily along their balconies they cry to their gods for succor. They arise, and from their windows they offer me their priceless household treasures — the sacred vessels dedicated to their great god Shiv — which they call 'Shivin Mugs' — the Kloes Brösh, the Boo-jak, urging me to fly them! And yet," said Miaow mournfully, "it is but my love-song! Think ye what they would do if I were on the war-path."

Another dead silence fell on the pool. Then arose that strange, mysterious, indefinable Thing, known as "The Scent." The animals sniffed.

"It heralds the approach of the Stalkies — the most famous of British Skool Boaz," said the Moo Kow. "They have just placed a decaying guinea-pig, two white mice in an advanced state of decomposition, and a single slice of Lim-

burger cheese in the bed of their tutor.
They had previously skillfully diverted
the drains so that they emptied into the
drawing-room of the head-master. They
have just burned down his house in an
access of noble zeal, and are fighting
among themselves for the spoil. Hark!
do ye hear them?"

A wild medley of shrieks and howls had
arisen, and an irregular mob of strange
creatures swept out of the distance toward
the pool. Some were like pygmies, some
had bloody noses. Their talk consisted of
feverish, breathless ejaculations, — a gib-
berish in which the words "rot," "oach,"
and "giddy" were preëminent. Some
were exciting themselves by chewing a
kind of "bhang" made from the plant
called pappahmint; others had their faces
streaked with djam.

"But who is this they are ducking in
the pool?" asked Pi Böl.

"It is one who has foolishly and wantonly conceived that his parents have sent him here to study," said the Moo Kow; "but that is against the rules of the Stalkies, who accept study only as a punishment."

"Then these be surely the 'Bander Log' — the monkey folk — of whom the good Rhuddyidd has told us," said a Gee Gee — "the ones who have no purpose — and forget everything."

"Fool!" said the Moo Kow. "Know ye not that the great Rhuddyidd has said that the Stalkies become Major-Generals, V. C.'s, and C. B's of the English? Truly, they are great. Look now; ye shall see one of the greatest traits of the English Stalky."

One of the pygmy Stalkies was offering a bun to a larger one, who hesitated, but took it coldly.

"Behold! it is one of the greatest traits of this mighty race not to show any emotion. He *would* take the bun — he *has* taken it! He is pleased — but he may not show it. Observe him eat."

The taller Stalky, after eating the bun, quietly kicked the giver, knocked off his hat, and turned away with a calm, immovable face.

"Good!" said the Moo Kow. "Ye would not dream that he was absolutely choking with grateful emotion?"

"We would not," said the animals.

"But why are they all running back the way they came?" asked Pi Böl.

"They are going back to punishment. Great is its power. Have ye not heard the gospel of Rhuddyidd the mighty? 'Force is everything! Gentleness won't wash, courtesy is deceitful. Politeness is foreign. Be ye beaten that ye may beat. Pass the kick on.'"

But here he was interrupted by the appearance of three soldiers who were approaching the watering-place.

"Ye are now," said the Moo Kow,

" with the main guard. The first is
Bleareyed, who carries a raven in a cage,
which he has stolen from the wife of a
deputy commissioner. He will paint the
bird snow white and sell it as a dove to the
same lady. The second is Otherwise, who
is dragging a small garden engine, of
which he has despoiled a native gardener,
whom he has felled with a single blow.
The third is Mulledwiney, swinging a cut-
glass decanter of sherry which he has just
snatched from the table of his colonel.
Mulledwiney and Otherwise will play the
engine upon Bleareyed, who is suffering
from heat apoplexy and djim-djams."

The three soldiers seated themselves in
the pool.

" They are going to tell awful war
stories now," said the Moo Kow, " stories
that are large and strong ! Some people
are shocked — others like 'em."

Then he that was called Mulledwiney
told a story. In the middle of it Miaow

got up from the limb of the tree, coughed slightly, and put her paw delicately over her mouth. " You must excuse me," she said faintly. " I am taken this way sometimes — and I have left my salts at home. Thanks ! I can get down myself ! " The next moment she had disappeared, but was heard coughing in the distance.

Mulledwiney winked at his companions and continued his story : —

" Wid that we wor in the thick av the foight. Whin I say 'thick' I mane it, sorr ! We wor that jammed together, divil a bit cud we shoot or cut ! At furrest, I had lashed two mushkits together wid the baynits out so, like a hay fork, and getting the haymaker's lift on thim, I just lifted two Paythians out — one an aych baynit — and passed 'em, aisy-like, over me head to the rear rank for them to finish. But what wid the blud gettin' into me ois, I was blinded, and the pressure kept incraysin' until me arrums was thrussed like a fowl to me sides, and sorra a bit cud I move but me jaws!"

"And bloomin' well you knew how to use them," said Otherwise.

"Thrue for you — though ye don't mane it!" said Mulledwiney, playfully tapping Otherwise on the head with a decanter till the cut glass slowly shivered. "So, begorra! there wor nothing left for me to do but to *ate* thim! Wirra! but it was the crooel worruk."

"Excuse me, my lord," interrupted the gasping voice of Pi Böl as he began to back from the pool, "I am but a horse, I know, and being built in that way — naturally have the stomach of one — yet, really, my lord, this — er " — And his voice was gone.

The next moment he had disappeared. Mulledwiney looked around with affected concern.

"Save us! But we 've cleaned out

the Jungle! Sure, there's not a baste
left but ourselves!"

It was true. The watering-place was
empty. Moo Kow, Miaow, and the Gee
Gees had disappeared. Presently there
was a booming crash and a long, deep
rumbling among the distant hills. Then
they knew they were near the old Moul-
mein Pagoda, and the dawn had come up
like thunder out of China 'cross the bay.
It always came up that way there. The
strain was too great, and day was actually
breaking.

"ZUT–SKI"

THE PROBLEM OF A WICKED FEME SOLE

By M–R–E C–R–LLI

" ZUT-SKI "

I

THE great pyramid towered up from
the desert with its apex toward the moon
which hung in the sky. For centuries
it had stood thus, disdaining the aid of
gods or man, being, as the Sphinx herself
observed, able to stand up for itself. And
this was no small praise from that sublime yet mysterious female who had seen
the ages come and go, empires rise and
fall, novelist succeed novelist, and who,
for eons and cycles the cynosure and
centre of admiration and men's idolatrous
worship, had yet — wonderful for a woman — through it all kept her head,
which now alone remained to survey
calmly the present. Indeed, at that moment that magnificent and peaceful face

seemed to have lost — with a few unimportant features — its usual expression of speculative wisdom and intense disdain ; its mouth smiled, its left eyelid seemed to droop. As the opal tints of dawn deepened upon it, the eyelid seemed to droop lower, closed, and quickly recovered itself twice. You would have thought the Sphinx had winked.

Then arose a voice like a wind on the desert, — but really from the direction of the Nile, where a hired dahabiyeh lay moored to the bank, — " 'Arry Axes ! 'Arry Axes ! " With it came also a flapping, trailing vision from the water — the sacred Ibis itself — and with wings aslant drifted mournfully away to its own creaking echo : " K'raksis ! K'raksis ! " Again arose the weird voice : " 'Arry Axes ! Wotcher doin' of ? " And again the Ibis croaked its wild refrain : "K'raksis ! K'raksis ! " Moonlight and the hour wove their own mystery (for which the author is not responsible), and the voice was heard no more. But when the full day sprang in glory over the desert, it illuminated the few remaining but sufficiently large features of the Sphinx with a burning saffron radiance! The Sphinx had indeed blushed!

II

I⊤ was the full season at Cairo. The wealth and fashion of Bayswater, South Kensington, and even the bosky Wood of the Evangelist had sent their latest luxury and style to flout the tombs of the past with the ghastly flippancy of to-day. The cheap tripper was there — the latest example of the Darwinian theory — ape-like, flea and curio hunting ! Shamelessly inquisitive and always hungry, what did he know of the Sphinx or the pyramids or the voice — and, for the matter of that, what did they know of him ? And yet he was not half bad in comparison with the "swagger people," — these people who pretend to have lungs and what not, and instead of galloping on merry hunters through the frost and snow of Piccadilly and Park, instead of enjoying the roaring fires of piled logs in the evening, at the first approach of winter steal away to the Land of the Sun, and decline to die, like honest Britons, on British soil. And then they know nothing of the Egyptians and are horrified at "bakshish," which they really ought to pay for the privilege of shocking the straight-limbed, naked-footed Arab in his single rough garment with their baggy elephant-legged trousers! And they know nothing of the mystic land of the old gods, filled with profound enigmas of the supernatural, dark secrets yet unexplored except in this book. Well might the great Memnon murmur after this lapse of these thousand years, "They 're making me tired!"

Such was the blissful, self-satisfied ignorance of Sir Midas Pyle, or as Lord Fitz-Fulke, with his delightful imitation of the East London accent, called him, Sir "Myde His Pyle," as he leaned back on his divan in the Grand Cairo Hotel. He was the vulgar editor and proprietor of a vulgar London newspaper, and had brought his wife with him, who was vainly trying to marry off his faded daughters. There was to be a fancy-dress ball at the hotel that night, and Lady Pyle hoped that her girls, if properly disguised, might have a better chance. Here, too, was Lady Fitz-Fulke, whose mother was immortalized by Byron — sixty if a day, yet still dressing youthfully — who had sought the land of the Sphinx in the faint hope that in the contiguity of that lady she might pass for being young. Alaster McFeckless, a splendid young Scotchman, — already dressed as a Florentine sailor of the fifteenth century, which enabled him to show his magnificent calves quite as well as in his native highland dress, and who had added with characteristic noble pride a sporran to his costume, — was lolling on another divan.

"Oh, those exquisite, those magnificent eyes of hers! Eh, sirs!" he murmured suddenly, as waking from a dream.

"Oh, damn her eyes!" said Lord Fitz-Fulke languidly. "Tell you what, old man, you're just gone on that girl!"

"Ha!" roared McFeckless, springing to his feet, "ye will be using such language of the bonniest"—

"You will excuse me, gentlemen," said Sir Midas, — who hated scenes unless he had a trusted reporter with him, — "but I think it is time for me to go upstairs and put on my Windsor uniform, which I find exceedingly convenient for these mixed assemblies." He withdrew, caressing his protuberant paunch with some dignity, as the two men glanced fiercely at each other.

In another moment they might have sprung at each other's throats. But luckily at this instant a curtain was pushed aside as if by some waiting listener, and

14—v. 5

a thin man entered, dressed in cap and gown, — which would have been simply academic but for his carrying in one hand behind him a bundle of birch twigs. It was Dr. Haustus Pilgrim, a noted London practitioner and specialist, dressed as " Ye Olde-fashioned Pedagogue." He was presumably spending his holiday on the Nile in a large dahabiyeh with a number of friends, among whom he counted the two momentary antagonists he had just interrupted ; but those who knew the doctor's far-reaching knowledge and cryptic researches believed he had his own scientific motives.

The two men turned quickly as he entered ; the angry light faded from their eyes, and an awed and respectful submission to the intruder took its place. He walked quietly toward them, put a lozenge in the mouth of one and felt the pulse of the other, gazing critically at both.

" We will be all right in a moment," he said with professional confidence.

" I say ! " said Fitz-Fulke, gazing at the doctor's costume, " you look dooced smart in those togs, don'tcherknow."

" They suit me," said the doctor, with a playful swish of his birch twigs, at which the two grave men shuddered. " But you were speaking of somebody's beautiful eyes."

" The Princess Zut-Ski's," returned McFeckless eagerly ; " and this daft callant said " —

" He did n't like them," put in Fitz-Fulke promptly.

" Ha ! " said the doctor sharply, " and why not, sir ? " As Fitz-Fulke hesitated, he added brusquely : "There ! Run away and play ! I 've business with this young man," pointing to McFeckless.

As Fitz-Fulke escaped gladly from the room, the doctor turned to McFeckless. " It won't do, my boy. The Princess is not for you — you 'll only break your heart and ruin your family over her ! That 's my advice. Chuck her ! "

" But I cannot," said McFeckless humbly. " Think of her weirdly beautiful eyes."

" I see," said the doctor meditatively ; "sort of makes you feel creepy ? Kind of all-overishness, eh ? That 's like her. But whom have we here ? "

He was staring at a striking figure that had just entered, closely followed by a crowd of admiring spectators. And, indeed, he seemed worthy of the homage. His magnificent form was closely attired in a velveteen jacket and trousers, with a singular display of pearl buttons along the seams, that were absolutely lavish in their quantity ; a hat adorned with feathers and roses completed his singularly picturesque equipment.

" Chevalier ! " burst out McFeckless in breathless greeting.

" Ah, *mon ami !* What good chance ? " returned the newcomer, rushing to him and kissing him on both cheeks, to the

British horror of Sir Midas, who had followed. "Ah, but you are perfect!" he added, kissing his fingers in admiration of McFeckless's Florentine dress.

"But you? — what is this ravishing costume?" asked McFeckless, with a pang of jealousy. "You are god-like."

"It is the dress of what you call the Koster, a transplanted Phenician tribe," answered the other. "They who knocked 'em in the road of Old Kent — know you not the legend?" As he spoke, he lifted his superb form to a warrior's height and gesture.

"But is this quite correct?" asked Fitz-Fulke of the doctor.

"Perfectly," said the doctor oracularly. "The renowned ''Arry Axes' — I beg his pardon," he interrupted himself hastily, "I mean the Chevalier — is perfect in his archæology and ethnology. The Koster is originally a Gypsy, which is but a corruption of the word 'Egyptian,' and, if I mistake not, that gentleman is a lineal descendant."

"But he is called 'Chevalier,' and he speaks like a Frenchman," said Fluffy.

"And, being a Frenchman, of course knows nothing outside of Paris," said Sir Midas.

"We are in the Land of Mystery," said the doctor gravely in a low voice. "You have heard of the Egyptian Hall and the Temple of Mystery?"

A shudder passed through many that were there; but the majority were following with wild adulation the superb Koster, who, with elbows slightly outward and hands turned inward, was passing toward the ballroom. McFeckless accompanied him with conflicting emotions. Would he see the incomparable Princess, who was lovelier and even still more a mystery than the Chevalier? Would she — terrible thought! — succumb to his perfections?

III

THE Princess was already there, surrounded by a crowd of admirers, equal if not superior to those who were following the superb Chevalier. Indeed, they met almost as rivals! Their eyes sought each other in splendid competition. The Chevalier turned away, dazzled and incoherent. "She is adorable, magnificent!" he gasped to McFeckless. "I love her on the instant! Behold, I am transported, ravished! Present me."

Indeed, as she stood there in a strange gauzy garment of exquisite colors, apparently shapeless, yet now and then revealing her perfect figure like a bather seen through undulating billows, she was lovely. Two wands were held in her taper fingers, whose mystery only added

to the general curiosity, but whose weird
and cabalistic uses were to be seen later.
Her magnificent face — strange in its
beauty — was stranger still, since, with
perfect archæological Egyptian correct-
ness, she presented it only in profile, at
whatever angle the spectator stood.   But
such a profile !   The words of the great
Poet - King rose to McFeckless's lips :
" Her nose is as a tower that looketh
toward Damascus."

He hesitated a moment, torn with love
and jealousy, and then presented his
friend.   " You will fall in love with her
— and then — you will fall also by my
hand," he hissed in his rival's ear, and
fled tumultuously.

" *Voulez-vous danser, mademoiselle ?* "
whispered the Chevalier in the perfect
accent of the boulevardier.

"*Merci, beaucoup,*" she replied in the
diplomatic courtesies of the Ambassadeurs.

They danced together, not once, but

many times, to the admiration, the wonder
and envy of all ; to the scandalized repro-
bation of a proper few. Who was she?
Who was he? It was easy to answer the
last question : the world rang with the
reputation of " Chevalier the Artist."
But she was still a mystery.

Perhaps they were not so to each other !
He was gazing deliriously into her eyes.
She was looking at him in disdainful
curiosity. " I've seen you before somewhere, have n't I ? " she said at last, with
a crushing significance.

He shuddered, he knew not why, and
passed his hand over his high forehead.
" Yes, I go there very often," he replied
vacantly. " But you, mademoiselle —
you — I have met before ? "

" Oh, ages, ages ago ! " There was
something weird in her emphasis.

" Ha ! " said a voice near them, " I
thought so ! " It was the doctor, peering
at them curiously. " And you both feel

rather dazed and creepy ? " He suddenly
felt their pulses, lingering, however, as the
Chevalier fancied, somewhat longer than
necessary over the lady's wrist and beautiful arm. He then put a small round box
in the Chevalier's hand, saying, " One
before each meal," and turning to the
lady with caressing professional accents
said, " We must wrap ourselves closely
and endeavor to induce perspiration,"
and hurried away, dragging the Chevalier
with him. When they reached a secluded
corner, he said, " You had just now a
kind of feeling, don't you know, as if
you 'd sort of been there before, did n't
you?"

" Yes, what you call a — preëxistence,"
said the Chevalier wonderingly.

" Yes; I have often observed that those
who doubt a future state of existence have
no hesitation in accepting a previous one,"
said the doctor dryly. " But come, I see
from the way the crowd are hurrying that

your divinity's number is up — I mean,"
he corrected himself hastily, " that she is
probably dancing again."

" Aha ! with him, the imbecile McFeckless ? " gasped the Chevalier.

" No, alone."

She was indeed alone, in the centre
of the ballroom —with outstretched arms
revolving in an occult, weird, dreamy,
mystic, druidical, cabalistic circle. They
now for the first time perceived the meaning of those strange wands which appeared
to be attached to the many folds of her
diaphanous skirts and involved her in a
fleecy, whirling cloud. Yet in the wild
convolutions of her garments and the mad
gyrations of her figure, her face was
upturned with the seraphic intensity of
a devotee, and her lips parted as with
the impassioned appeal for " Light ! more
light ! " And the appeal was answered.
A flood of blue, crimson, yellow, and
green radiance was alternately poured

upon her from the black box of a
mysterious Nubian slave in the gallery.
The effect was marvelous ; at one moment
she appeared as a martyr in a sheet of
flame, at another as an angel wrapped in
white and muffled purity, and again as
a nymph of the cerulean sea, and then
suddenly a cloud of darkness seemed to
descend upon her, through which for an
instant her figure, as immaculate and perfect as a marble statue, showed distinctly
— then the light went out and she vanished !

The whole assembly burst into a rap-
turous cry.   Even the common Arab at-
tendants who were peeping in at the doors
raised their melodious native cry, " Alloe,
Fullah ! Alloe, Fullah ! " again and again.

A shocked silence followed.   Then the
voice of Sir Midas Pyle was heard addressing Dr. Haustus Pilgrim :

" May we not presume, sir, that what
we have just seen is not unlike that re-

markable exhibition when I was pained to meet you one evening at the Alhambra?"

The doctor coughed slightly. "The Alhambra — ah, yes ! — you — er — refer, I presume, to Granada and the Land of the Moor, where we last met. The music and dance are both distinctly Moorish — which, after all, is akin to the Egyptian. I am gratified indeed that your memory should be so retentive and your archæological comparison so accurate. But see ! the ladies are retiring. Let us follow."

IV

THE intoxication produced by the performance of the Princess naturally had its reaction. The British moral soul, startled out of its hypocrisy the night before, demanded the bitter beer of self-consciousness and remorse the next morning. The ladies were now openly shocked at what they had secretly envied. Lady Pyle was, however, propitiated by the doctor's assurance that the Princess was a friend of Lady Fitz-Fulke, who had promised to lend her youthful age and aristocratic prestige to the return ball which the Princess had determined to give at her own home. "Still, I think the Princess open to criticism," said Sir Midas oracularly.

"Damn all criticism and critics!" burst

out McFeckless, with the noble frankness
of a passionate and yet unfettered soul.
Sir Midas, who employed critics in his
business, as he did other base and ignoble
slaves, drew up himself and his paunch
and walked away.

The Chevalier cast a superb look at
McFeckless. " *Voilà!* Regard me well!
I shall seek out this Princess when she is
with herself! Alone, *comprenez?* I shall
seek her at her hotel in the Egyptian
Hall! Ha! ha! I shall seek Zut-Ski!
Zut!" And he made that rapid yet graceful motion of his palm against his thigh
known only to the true Parisian.

" It's a rum hole where she lives, and
nobody gets a sight of her," said Flossy.
" It's like a beastly family vault, don't
you know, outside, and there's a kind of
nigger doorkeeper that visés you and
chucks you out if you have n't the straight
tip. I'll show you the way, if you like."

" *Allons, en avant!*" said the Chevalier gayly. " I precipitate myself there on the instant."

" Remember ! " hissed McFeckless, grasping his arm, " you shall account to me ! "

" *Bien !* " said the Chevalier, shaking him off lightly. " All a-r-r-right." Then, in that incomparable baritone, which had so often enthralled thousands, he moved away, trolling the first verse of the Princess's own faint, sweet, sad song of the " Lotus Lily," that thrilled McFeckless even through the Chevalier's marked French accent : —

" Oh, a hard zing to get is ze Lotus Lillee !
  She lif in ze swamp — in ze watair chillee ;
  She make your foot wet — and you look so sillee,
  But you buy her for sixpence in Piccadillee ! "

In half an hour the two men reached the remote suburb where the Princess lived, a gloomy, windowless building. Pausing under a low archway over which in Egyptian characters appeared the faded legend, " Sta Ged Oor," they found a Nubian slave blocking the dim entrance.

" I leave you here," said Flossy hurriedly, " as even I left once before — only then I was lightly assisted by his sandaled foot," he added, rubbing himself thoughtfully. " But better luck to you."

As his companion retreated swiftly, the Chevalier turned to the slave and would have passed in, but the man stopped him. " Got a pass, boss ? "

" No," said the Chevalier.

The man looked at him keenly. " Oh, I see ! one of de profesh."

The Chevalier nodded haughtily. The man preceded him by devious, narrow ways and dark staircases, coming abruptly upon a small apartment where the Princess sat on a low divan. A single lamp inclosed in an ominous wire cage flared above her. Strange things lay about the floor and shelves, and from another door he could see hideous masks, frightful heads, and disproportionate faces. He shuddered slightly, but recovered himself and fell on his knees before her. "I lofe you," he said madly. "I have always lofed you!"

"For how long?" she asked, with a strange smile.

He covertly consulted his shirt cuff. "For tree tousand fife hundred and sixty-two years," he said rapidly.

She looked at him disdainfully. "The doctor has been putting you up to that! It won't wash! I don't refer to your shirt cuff," she added with deep satire.

"Adorable one!" he broke out passionately, attempting to embrace her, "I have come to take you." Without moving, she touched a knob in the wall. A trap-door beyond him sank, and out of the bowels of the earth leaped three indescribable demons. Then, rising, she took a cake of chalk from the table and, drawing a mystic half circle on the floor, returned to the divan, lit a cigarette, and leaning comfortably back, said in a low, monotonous voice, "Advance one foot within that magic line, and on that head, although it wore a crown, I launch the curse of Rome."

" I — only wanted to take you — with a kodak," he said, with a light laugh to conceal his confusion, as he produced the instrument from his coat-tail pocket.

" Not with that cheap box," she said, rising with magnificent disdain. " Come again with a decent instrument — and perhaps " — Then, lightly humming in a pure contralto, " I 've been photographed like this — I 've been photographed like that," she summoned the slave to conduct him back, and vanished through a canvas screen, which nevertheless seemed to the dazed Chevalier to be the stony front of the pyramids.

V

"AND you saw her?" said the doctor in French.

"Yes; but the three-thousand-year gag did not work! She spotted you, *cher ami*, on the instant. And she would n't let me take her with my kodak."

The doctor looked grave. "I see," he mused thoughtfully. "You must have my camera, a larger one and more bulky perhaps to carry; but she will not object to that, — she who has stood for full lengths. I will give you some private instructions."

"But, *cher* doctor, this previous-existence idea — at what do you arrive?"

"There is much to say for it," said the doctor oracularly. "It has survived in the belief of all ages. Who can tell?

That some men in a previous existence
may have been goats or apes," continued
the doctor, looking at him curiously, "does
not seem improbable ! From the time of
Pythagoras we have known that ; but that
the individual as an individual ego has
been remanded or projected, has harked
back or anticipated himself, is, we may say,
with our powers of apperception, — that
is, the perception that we are perceiving,
— is " —

But the Chevalier had fled. "No matter," said the doctor, "I will see McFeckless." He did. He found him gloomy,
distraught, baleful. He felt his pulse.
"The mixture as before," he said briefly,
"and a little innocent diversion. There
is an Aunt Sally on the esplanade — two
throws for a penny. It will do you good.
Think no more of this woman ! Listen,
— I wish you well ; your family have
always been good patients of mine. Marry
some good Scotch girl ; I know one with

fifty thousand pounds. Let the Princess go!"

"To him — never! I will marry her! Yet," he murmured softly to himself, "feefty thousand pun' is nae small sum. Aye! Not that I care for siller — but feefty thousand pun'! Eh, sirs!"

VI

Dr. Haustus knew that the Chevalier had again visited the Princess, although he had kept the visit a secret, — and indeed was himself invisible for a day or two afterwards. At last the doctor's curiosity induced him to visit the Chevalier's apartment. Entering, he was surprised — even in that Land of Mystery — to find the room profoundly dark, smelling of Eastern drugs, and the Chevalier sitting before a large plate of glass which he was examining by the aid of a lurid ruby lamp, — the only light in the weird gloom. His face was pale and distraught, his locks were disheveled.

"*Voilà!*" he said. "*Mon Dieu!* It is my third attempt. Always the same — hideous, monstrous, unearthly! It is she, and yet it is not she!"

The doctor, professional man as he was and inured to such spectacles, was startled! The plate before him showed the Princess's face in all its beautiful contour, but only dimly veiling a ghastly death's-head below. There was the whole bony structure of the head and the eyeless sockets; even the graceful, swan-like neck showed the articulated vertebral column that supported it in all its hideous reality. The beautiful shoulders were there, dimly as in a dream — but beneath was the empty clavicle, the knotty joint, the hollow sternum, and the ribs of a skeleton half length!

The doctor's voice broke the silence. "My friend," he said dryly, "you see only the truth! You see what she really is, this peerless Princess of yours. You see her as she is to-day, and you see her kinship to the bones that have lain for centuries in yonder pyramid. Yet they were once as fair as this, and this was as fair as they — in effect the same! **You** that have madly, impiously adored her superficial beauty, the mere dust of tomorrow, let this be a warning to you! You that have no soul to speak of, let that suffice you! Take her and be happy. Adieu!"

Yet, as he passed out of the fitting tomblike gloom of the apartment and descended the stairs, he murmured to himself: "Odd that I should have lent him my camera with the Röntgen-ray attachment still on. No matter! It is not the first time that the Princess has appeared in two parts the same evening."

VII

In spite of envy, jealousy, and malice, a certain curiosity greater than all these drew everybody to the Princess Zut-Ski's ball. Lady Fitz-Fulke was there in virgin white, looking more youthful than ever, in spite of her sixty-five years and the card labeled "Fresh Paint" which somebody had playfully placed upon her enameled shoulder. The McFecklesses, the Pyles, Flossy, the doctor, and the Chevalier — looking still anxious — were in attendance.

The mysterious Nubian doorkeeper admitted the guests through the same narrow passages, much to the disgust of Lady Pyle and the discomfiture of her paunchy husband; but on reaching a large circular interior hall, a greater surprise was in store for them. It was found that the only entrance to the body of the hall was along a narrow ledge against the bare wall some distance from the floor, which obliged the guests to walk slowly, in single file, along this precarious strip, giving them the attitudes of an Egyptian frieze, which was suggested in the original plaster above them. It is needless to say that, while the effect was ingenious and striking from the centre of the room, where the Princess stood with a few personal friends, it was exceedingly uncomfortable to the figures themselves, in their enforced march along the ledge, — especially a figure of Sir Midas Pyle's proportions. Suddenly an exclamation broke from the doctor.

"Do you see," he said to the Princess, pointing to the figure of the Chevalier, who was filing along with his sinewy hands slightly turned inward, "how surprisingly like he is to the first attendant on the King in the real frieze above? And that," added the doctor, " was none other than 'Arry Axes, the Egyptian you are always thinking of." And he peered curiously at her.

" Goodness me ! " murmured the Princess, in an Arabic much more soft and fluent than the original gum. " So he does — look like him."

" And do you know you look like him, too ? Would you mind taking a walk around together ? "

They did, amid the acclamations of the crowd. The likeness was perfect. The Princess, however, was quite white as she eagerly rejoined the doctor.

" And this means — ? " she hissed in a low whisper.

" That he is the real 'Arry Axes ! Hush, not a word now ! We join the dahabiyeh to-night. At daybreak you will meet him at the fourth angle of the pyramid, first turning from the Nile ! "

VIII

THE crescent moon hung again over the apex of the Great Pyramid, like a silver cutting from the rosy nail of a houri. The Sphinx — mighty guesser of riddles, reader of rebuses and universal solver of missing words — looked over the unfathomable desert and these few pages, with the worried, hopeless expression of one who is obliged at last to give it up. And then the wailing voice of a woman, toiling up the steep steps of the pyramid, was heard above the creaking of the Ibis: "'Arry Axes! Where are you? Wait for me."

"*J'y suis*," said a voice from the very summit of the stupendous granite bulk, "yet I cannot reach it."

And in that faint light the figure of a

man was seen, lifting his arms wildly toward the moon.

"'Arry Axes," persisted the voice, drifting higher, "wait for me; we are pursued."

And indeed it was true. A band of Nubians, headed by the doctor, was already swarming like ants up the pyramid, and the unhappy pair were secured. And when the sun rose, it was upon the white sails of the dahabiyeh, the vacant pyramid, and the slumbering Sphinx.

There was great excitement at the Cairo Hotel the next morning. The Princess and the Chevalier had disappeared, and with them Alaster McFeckless, Lady Fitz-Fulke, the doctor, and even his dahabiyeh! A thousand rumors had been in circulation. Sir Midas Pyle looked up from the "Times" with his usual I-told-you-so expression.

"It is the most extraordinary thing,

don'tcherknow," said Fitz-Fulke. "It
seems that Dr. Haustus Pilgrim was here
professionally — as a nerve specialist — in
the treatment of hallucinations produced
by neurotic conditions, you know."

"A mad doctor, here!" gasped Sir
Midas.

"Yes. The Princess, the Chevalier,
McFeckless, and even my mother were all
patients of his on the dahabiyeh. He
believed, don'tcherknow, in humoring
them and letting them follow out their
cranks, under his management. The
Princess was a music-hall artist who imagined she was a dead and gone Egyptian
Princess; and the queerest of all, 'Arry
Axes was also a music-hall singer who
imagined himself Chevalier — you know,
the great Koster artist — and that's how
we took him for a Frenchman. McFeckless and my poor old mother were the
only ones with any real rank and position
— but you know what a beastly bounder

Mac was, and the poor mater *did* overdo the youthful! We never called the doctor in until the day she wanted to go to a swell ball in London as Little Red Ridinghood. But the doctor writes me that the experiment was a success, and they'll be all right when they get back to London."

"Then, it seems, sir, that you and I were the only sane ones here," said Sir Midas furiously.

"Really it's as much as I can do to be certain about myself, old chappie," said Fitz-Fulke, turning away.

THE END